ROGER FOWLER

LINGUISTICS AND THE NOVEL

ROUTLEDGE
LONDON and NEW YORK

First published in 1977 by
Methuen & Co. Ltd
Reprinted 1979
Reprinted with revisions 1983
Reprinted 1985

Reprinted 1989
by Routledge
11 New Fetter Lane, London EC4P 4EE
29 West 35th Street, New York, NY 10001

© *1977 Roger Fowler*

Printed in Great Britain by
T. J. Press (Padstow)
Ltd, Padstow, Cornwall

ISBN 0 416 83820 0 (hardback edition)
ISBN 0 415 04293 3 (paperback edition)

CONTENTS

GENERAL EDITOR'S PREFACE

IT is easy to see that we are living in a time of rapid radical social change. It is much less easy to grasp the fact that such change will inevitably affect the nature of those disciplines that both reflect our society and help to shape it.

Yet this is nowhere more apparent than in the central field of what may, in general terms, be called literary studies. Here, among large numbers of students at all levels of education, the erosion of the assumptions and presuppositions that support the literary disciplines in their conventional form has proved fundamental. Modes and categories inherited from the past no longer seem to fit the reality experienced by a new generation.

New Accents is intended as a positive response to the initiative offered by such a situation. Each volume in the series will seek to encourage rather than resist the process of change, to stretch rather than reinforce the boundaries that currently define literature and its academic study.

Some important areas of interest will obviously be those in which an initial impetus seems to come from linguistics. As its title suggests, one aspect of *New Accents* will be firmly located in contemporary approaches to language, and a central concern of the series will be to examine the extent to which relevant branches of linguistic studies can illuminate specific literary areas. The volumes with this particular interest will nevertheless presume no prior technical knowledge on the part of their readers, and will aim to expound the linguistics appropriate to the matter in hand, rather than to embark on general theoretical matters.

Modern linguistics has also provided a basis for the study of the totality of human communication, and so ultimately for an analysis of the human role in the world at large. It seems appropriate, therefore, that the series should also concern itself with those wider anthropological and sociological areas of investigation which, deriving from the linguistic model, ultimately involve scrutiny of the nature of art itself and of its relation to our whole way of life.

This in turn will require attention to be focused on some of those activities which in our society have hitherto been excluded from the prestigious realms of Culture. The disturbing realignment of values which this involves, and the disconcerting nature of the pressures that work to bring it about both constitute areas that *New Accents* will seek to explore.

Each volume in the series will attempt an objective exposition of significant developments in its field up to the present as well as an account of its author's own views of the matter. Each will culminate in an informative bibliography as a guide to further study. And while each will be primarily concerned with matters relevant to its own specific interests, we can hope that a kind of conversation will be heard to develop between them: one whose accents may perhaps suggest the distinctive discourse of the future.

TERENCE HAWKES

PREFACE

THERE are a number of recent developments in and around linguistics which deserve to be better known to literary critics, for they point to original ways of reading and analysis; and literary criticism, as a discipline, has always welcomed innovation. Some of these developments suggest to me a new approach in the criticism of fiction, and in the present book I have attempted to draw together several threads in a preliminary sketch of the new method. I have been very eclectic, drawing on several approaches.

Chomsky's transformational grammar provides an interpretation of the traditional notion of 'style' as a relationship between meaning and expression. Halliday's 'functional' approach encourages us to think about *why* a language-user chooses one sentence-structure rather than an alternative, and Halliday provides some valuable terminology for our answers to such questions. I will be using these modes of linguistic description to focus particularly on the ways individual sentences add up to a larger textual shape; on their power to suggest distinctive 'mind-styles' in authors and characters; and on the relationships between 'voices' within the novel – a topic suggestively treated in the writings of a school of Russian linguist-critics founded by Mikhail Bakhtin in the 1930s. Their major work is now available in English, and is strongly recommended.

The main preoccupation of the present book is the significance, for the novel-reader and critic, of sentence-structures, and of 'transformations,' both in the individual sentence and cumulatively in a complete work. That is to say, my descriptive analyses, and generalizations from them, are based on an established (though unconventionally eclectic) model of 'sentence-linguistics'. But I see this kind of study as, ultimately, only one part, if the most important, of a linguistic theory of the narrative text. Contemporary linguistics is moving to a realization that it must extend its scope beyond the traditional domain of the sentence to take in the structure of whole texts. This new 'text-linguistics' – being developed mainly in the Netherlands and Germany – is still very programmatic, and tentative in the detail of its proposals. I have drawn some general ideas from text-grammar. Assuming that a text has an overall structure analogous to that of a single sentence, I have derived from this analogy some general structural notions such as 'discourse', to work in co-operation with established literary concepts of the 'elements' of the novel. Another example of my use of the analogy occurs in the analysis of 'character' and 'theme' which draws on semantic features like those proposed for the descriptions of the meanings of single words (see pp. 33–41). Many other applications of the sentence/text analogy can be envisaged, but they are perhaps too ambitious for the present. For instance, one might conceive of deriving the surface structure of a whole text from an underlying 'theme' in the same fashion as a sentence surface structure is derived by a linguist from semantic 'deep structure'.

Text-grammar is compatible with another relevant current trend: the structural analysis of narrative and of myth as practised by French writers like Roland Barthes, Tzvetan Todorov and Claude Lévi-Strauss. Because structuralism is the subject of another volume in this series

(Terence Hawkes, *Structuralism and Semiotics*), I have made only cursory reference to it. I am not one of those Anglo-Saxon critics who maintain that French structuralism is merely intellectually frivolous, or absurdly reductionist. Describing plot structure and theme, and the roles of protagonists, in ways which relate these structures to potential universals, seem to me valid and important enterprises in the theory and history of the novel. My relative neglect is a simple case of division of labour.

The French distinguish two levels of literary structure, which they call *histoire* and *discours*, story and language. Story (or plot) and the other abstract elements of novel structure may be discussed in terms of categories given by the analogy of linguistic theory, but the *direct* concern of linguistics is surely with the study of *discours*. So I have referred to the general linguistic theory of narrative only as a means of supplying a framework within which my own work, on the language proper of fiction, has, I hope, a defined place. (For further discussion of the broader framework of linguistic-literary structuralism, see the books by Culler, Hawkes and Scholes cited on p. 139 below.)

I have also economized on space by omitting some other topics which manifestly belong to 'the language of fiction'. For instance, I have nothing to say about conventions for the representation of dialogue, or of dialect speech; no discussion of figurative language, e.g. thematically significant iterative metaphors; nothing on creatively deformed or deviant language of the *Finnegans Wake* kind. I don't regard these topics as unimportant, far from it: these aspects of language structure contribute immediately to style and tone. But their analysis doesn't demand a very sophisticated technical linguistics, and they have already been treated by such critics as Lodge and Page (see pp. 138 and 140 below). In this short book I have concentrated on topics which need a more advanced linguistics, and which demand that linguistics should be used progressively, not just as a source of descriptions that can be phrased just as well in critical language.

It becomes very clear to anyone working on the theory of fiction that the general statements about the novel one is prepared to commit oneself to depend on one's view of the *history* of prose fiction. What, for the critic and his reader, is the 'typical' novel? We are talking about a massive and highly diverse collection of works, written in many different circumstances over a period of more than two hundred years. There is no typical novel. The critic creates *his* typical novel by selecting from the literature, and by discussing his selections in the way he chooses. The theorist, knowing this, ought to be as explicit as he can about his version of the history and diversification of the novel. I don't have the space to furnish my history of the novel here, and I am conscious of many places in this book where qualifications and explanations have had to be skimped. I have tried to use expressions like 'many novelists' and 'usually' circumspectly, and can only hope that my implied ideal novel is not felt to be too eccentric or too archaic.

A word about the arrangement of this volume. The first two chapters introduce the major technical concepts used by the argument. Chapter 1 offers some relevant ideas from linguistics; chapter 2, a scheme of 'elements' of novelstructure derived from the linguistic categories. Chapters 3 and 4 consist largely of illustrative analyses within some of the areas of language structure defined earlier. Chapter 4, 'Discourse', also discusses topics which are closest to the centre of the linguistic study of the novel as I see it at the moment. Chapter 5 is intended as a brief conclusion and a prospect at the same time: it attempts to place the preceding material in perspective by offering an account of the role of structure for the individual reader and the community of novel-readers. It concludes by suggesting some lines for future work which might be based on this broader perspective.

Throughout the book my presentation of the material and of the case derived from it is cumulative or progressive. My position on this new subject is not authoritative or inflexible, and I have tried to give the reader a sense of flexible development by leading him through an argument which works itself out and modifies itself as it proceeds. The book is best read straight through the first time, and then perhaps re-read skipping forwards and backwards, applying different parts of the argument to passages I have quoted in another context.

While writing this book I have received invaluable help from students at the University of East Anglia in Britain, and at Brown University in America, who thrashed out many of the ideas with me in seminars; from Malcolm Bradbury and Terence Hawkes, who helped me remove confusions from early drafts; and from Lesley Nguyen and Muriel Utting, who did much of the typing. Peter Fowler helped me to correct the proofs.

1983 reprint

Linguistics and the Novel was offered in 1977 as an outline proposal for a new approach to the study of prose fiction. It could be amplified in many ways – for example a fuller treatment of the very programmatic suggestions of ch. 5 – but only by sacrificing the attractively compact *New Accents* format. I think the proposal as a whole is still valid. Wishing to preserve the general drift of the argument, I have avoided any temptation to tinker with details. I have however completely rewritten the section recommending further reading, which is now more informative, and updated to the end of 1982. I am indebted to my colleague Ellman Crasnow for advice on bringing my references up-to-date.

1 PRINCIPLES

Introduction: criticism, language and fiction

THIS little book offers a new perspective on the criticism, and therefore the reading, of novels and other forms of narrative prose: a viewpoint provided by *linguistics*. How does the current state of novel-criticism lead me to choose this perspective, the perspective of a science devoted so far to the study of 'ordinary language' and not originally designed to cope with extended fictional works?

Over the last two hundred years, the novel has become the dominant form of literary writing in most literate societies; in quantity (thousands of titles published every year in America and in Western Europe), readership consumption (verse and drama are now truly minority pleasures) and in cultural sensitivity (novels rapidly and significantly reflect, and help to shape, the socio-economic realities and the fantasies of their consumers). The novel is also the literary form most vitally in contact with other contemporaneous modes of discourse: with journalism, advertising, documentary, history, sociology, science and (in another medium) cinema. As the novel has become the most significant form of literary writing, its growth has coincided with the establishment of an age of literary-critical consciousness: 'literature' – a global concept unimagined in the value-loaded modern sense before the mid-nineteenth century – has become an established cultural institution, and 'criticism' is a massive secondary institution obligatory in universities, publishers' lists and newspapers.

Until very recently, criticism of the novel, and theories of the novel and its close relatives, were at a much more primitive level than the theory and criticism of poetry. Classical literary theories made no provision for the novel, since it was an unknown mode of writing; and when it did emerge, it didn't easily fit the surviving classical categories: it was not clearly epic, or lyric, or dramatic; or comic or tragic; or poetic, or philosophical, or historical. In 1742 Henry Fielding humorously captured the indefinite or chameleon status of the novel when he referred to his *Joseph Andrews* as 'a comic Epic-Poem in Prose'. Even today, some critics, doubtless influenced by the polymorphic, inclusive, quality of arch-modern novels such as *Ulysses* (1922) suggest that the essence of the genre is that it draws upon the forms of all and any genres. Others – and only in this century – have sought to devise a more specific 'poetics' for the novel form. The novelist Henry James, with the Prefaces to the New York edition of his novels (1907–17), stimulated long overdue interest in such technical aspects of the composition of narrative fiction as point of view and temporal foreshortening. A quarter of a century later, it was still necessary for Mark Schorer, in an essay called 'Technique as Discovery' (1948) * to insist on the primacy of technique in the expression of meanings and values in prose fiction – a principle long accepted in discussions of poetry. Wayne Booth's pioneering *Rhetoric of Fiction* appeared as recently as 1961. David Lodge's proposal, in *Language of Fiction* (1966), that the verbal analysis of New Criticism should be extended from poetry to the novel, seemed innovatory to some, yet the New Criticism had ceased to be a live critical programme

* See 'Further Reading', pp. 134–43, for this and other references.

at least a decade earlier. When Brown University started its periodical *Novel* in 1967, the magazine launched into a series called 'Towards a Poetics of Fiction' with the urgency of a zoologist hastening to record a vanishing species – for it was becoming fashionable to proclaim that the novel was dead or dying!

That dismal prognostication apart, there has been much (belated) creative theorizing and criticism on the technique of fiction in this century, and particularly in the last fifteen years or so. I stress the notion of 'technique' for several reasons. First, an attention to technique is the only foundation for an understanding of the nature of prose fictions, since they are inescapably artefacts, man-made objects with a place in a culture's technology and an individual's workmanly productivity. There is a dreadful tradition of vapid reviewing which treats novels as if they were unedited, uncrafted, windows on life – the reader is supposed to look straight through the words at the pictured characters and settings just as one peers out through a spotless pane on one's nextdoor neighbour. But the 'world out there' of the novel is an artifice constructed through the novelist's technique, and we must be inquisitive about the means by which this shaping takes place.

Second, a writer's technique is, immediately and ultimately, a craft in language: as Lodge says, 'the novelist's medium is language: whatever he does, *qua* novelist, he does in and through language'. The structure of the novel and whatever it communicates are under the direct control of the novelist's manipulation of language, and concomitantly, of the reader's recreative sympathy, his desire and ability to realize and release the technique from verbal clues deposited by the author. The linguistic character of novelistic technique is generally recognized by critics; so it would seem natural and desirable to submit the language of fiction to any of the processes and terms of linguistic analysis which appear appropriate to the tasks of criticism.

The naturalness of this application is enhanced if we conceive of linguistics not just as a device for formalistic analysis capable only of tracing the outline, texture and contours of a text, but as a mode of analysis which can suggest *interpretations* of structural form. Choices of words and sentence-types possess conventional reverberations, associations, for members of a reading community. If we employ a linguistics which is sensitive to these community associations of language (a linguistics which treats the sociological and psychological aspects of language), we can begin to interpret a writer's linguistic structures in relation to the values and preoccupations of the community for which he writes.

There is another, though not essential, reason why we should approach the novel primarily by way of technique, and desirably by way of linguistics. In this century, the novel has become the major medium for technical innovation in European and American literature, and the innovations are generally directly expressed in linguistic creativity. One immediately thinks of the new devices for rendering consciousness discovered by Henry James, Marcel Proust, Virginia Woolf, James Joyce, William Faulkner; of Joyce's triumphant and creative destruction and reconstruction of the language of the classical bourgeois novel in *Ulysses* (1922) and *Finnegans Wake* (1939), instituting a tradition rich in verbal play and carried on by Samuel Beckett, Vladimir Nabokov, John Barth and many slighter figures; of the experiments with structure and perspective made familiar by the work of the Argentinian Jorge Luis Borges and by the exponents of the French *nouveau roman*. Although experimentalism is not a novelty in the history of fiction, the strong insistence in much of this new writing on the linguistic nature of fiction itself is significant. These new techniques in prose fiction are a stimulus to structural criticism, and particularly to criticism closely engaged with language; so it has proved in France, where the writing of fiction and of criticism are now intimately interdependent, practised by a homogeneous group of affiliated people, and sharing many features of formal invention. One *nouveau roman* (written in English), whose subject-matter includes linguistics, will be discussed in chapter 3. The situation in France is of especial interest to the joining of linguistics and prose fiction, and I will make further reference to the French structuralists' ideas about language and the technique of fiction. Though French structuralism is not linguistics, it does comprise a theory of communication and, having the classical language-theory of Saussure as a prominent part of its formative background, makes substantial use of linguistic concepts.

Text and sentence

I shall now set out some of the linguistic equipment which this book will call upon in the analysis of fiction. What I have to say is rather abstract, and I would like to forestall one specific possible confusion by a clear warning at the outset. I will be discussing the structure of two separate types of unit, *sentences* and *texts*.

In certain circumstances a text may consist of a single sentence, e.g. proverbs ('A stitch in time saves nine') or notices ('Please switch off the light'). Ordinarily, however, we can think of texts as constructed out of sequences of sentences. A sentence is an element, or unit, or constituent of a text; a text is made out of sentences in a quite ordinary sense of 'made out of'. The potential confusion is not in this idea alone but in the following feature of my argument: I shall maintain that texts are structurally *like* sentences (as well as being constructed out of sentences). That is to say, the categories of structure that we propose for the analysis of individual sentences (in linguistics) can be extended to apply to the analysis of much larger structures in texts. The reasons for this strategy will be indicated below. The effect will be to speak of, for example, nouns as elements in sentence-structure and 'nouns' as elements in narrative structure; of the deep and surface structure of sentences and the 'deep' and 'surface' structure of texts. Since textual 'surface structure' consists of sentences, and sentences have their own surface and deep structures, there is some potential confusion here, but I hope that this will be substantially outweighed by the insights obtained from comparing text-structure with sentence-structure.

Deep structure and surface structure

In virtually every version of linguistic theory, a sentence is regarded as a combination of a 'form' and a 'content'. In modern transformational-generative grammar, the revolutionary style of grammar invented by Noam Chomsky, this is expressed as a pairing of a surface structure and a deep structure. Surface structure is the observable, or the expressive, layer of the sentence; most concretely, sound or written symbol; somewhat more abstractly, syntax: word- and phrase-order. Deep structure is the abstract content of the sentence: the *structure of meaning* which is being expressed. We experience surface structure directly, but retrieve deep structure, or meaning, only by a complex act of decoding.

Surface structure has important properties for the construction and reading of fiction. *Linearity* is one such property – sentences, but not their meanings, which are abstract, move from left to right in space or time, shifting the reader's attention along and sometimes impeding it. Linear sequence may be used to suggest narrative time, as in these sentences from Hemingway's *A Farewell to Arms* (1929):

> ... one of the doctors brought in Rinaldi. He came in very fast and bent down over the bed and kissed me. I saw he wore gloves.

The incident might have been expressed in quite some other

way, but this chosen sequence conveys movement through time. Note how the positioning of the final sentence, after the obviously time-sequential one, suggests that the gloves were seen at close quarters after the kiss, not distantly, e.g. on Rinaldi's first entry through the door: nothing *states* this chronological order, but it is implicit in the surface-structure linear sequence. In the following sentence, from Henry James's *Washington Square* (1881), the order of phrases imitates both the length of a block of time (a pause in a nervous dialogue), and the aimless wandering of visual attention:

'We must settle something – we must take a line,' he declared, passing his hand through his hair and giving a glance at the long, narrow mirror which adorned the space between the two windows, and which had at its base a little gilded bracket covered by a thin slab of white marble, supporting in its turn a backgammon-board folded together in the shape of two volumes – two shining folios inscribed, in greenish-gilt letters, *History of England.*

Again we are conscious that the elements here – action and description – could have been disposed in quite a different way, but without the same temporal insistence.

Surface structure also conveys logical relationships: it has ways of signalling differentials of importance among the parts of a complex system of meanings, and for picking out what is new information as contrasted with the already known, given or presupposed meanings communicated by a sentence. Consider, for example, the way in which the arrangement of clauses in the surface order of this very ordinary paragraph from George Eliot's *The Mill on the Floss* (1860) splits up the information given into its more and less prominent parts, focusing the reader's attention on the feel-ings and actions of Maggie Tulliver and subordinating what

are from the point of view of this particular narration in-
essential and contingent details:

> It was a heavy disappointment to Maggie that she was
> not allowed to go with her father in the gig when he went
> to fetch Tom home from the academy; but the morning
> was too wet, Mrs Tulliver said, for a little girl to go out
> in her best bonnet. Maggie took the opposite view very
> strongly, and it was a direct consequence of this differ-
> ence of opinion that when her mother was in the act of
> brushing out the reluctant black crop, Maggie suddenly
> rushed out from under her hands and dipped her head
> in a basin of water standing near – in the vindictive
> determination that there should be no more chance of
> curls that day.

The syntax manages to 'foreground' both the severity of
Maggie's feelings and the violence of her actions, and to
'background' their causes and their consequences. Two
crucial clauses are transformed into ponderously striking
noun phrases which can be placed in attention-catching 'left-
hand' syntactic positions – 'heavy disappointment' at the
beginning of the first sentence and 'vindictive determination' after the dash; contrast the less emphatic untrans-
formed versions 'Maggie was disappointed/vindictive/
determined'. In addition to this positional prominence, the
sonorous polysyllables of the words concerned also highlight
the importance of the meanings conveyed by them. (Poly-
syllabicity is of course very concrete, a pure feature of surface
structure.) In the first sentence, expression of the cause of
Maggie's disappointment dwindles out to the right in
subordinate clauses. For the remainder, Maggie has a
monopoly of active, finite verbs in prominent positions.
'Mrs Tulliver said' is parenthesized, placing the action of
saying below, in importance, even the feeble substance of
what she says. Contrast the active directness of the first
clause of the next sentence: 'Maggie took the opposite

view.' Actually, 'taking the opposite view' isn't an action, but the archetypal subject–verb–object sequence manages to suggest that it is, a surface-structure implication vindicated by the subsequent active finite verbs: 'Maggie suddenly rushed . . . and dipped her head in a basin of water . . .' The syntactic mechanisms of the centre of this sentence forewarn the reader that these major semantic nuclei are to come: 'it was a direct consequence . . . *that*' announces a main clause to come, and '*when* her mother was . . .' indicates clearly a suspension of major meaning for one more subordinate clause. By such devices the syntactic structure leads the reader through the semantic centres of the prose, emphasizing and playing down as appropriate.

For a contrast, consider how this sentence from James's *The Ambassadors* (1903) almost perversely conceals from the reader relationships of logic and of comparative significance, among the various facets of what is being said:

> What had come as straight to him as a ball in a well-played game – and caught moreover not less neatly – was just the air, in the person of his friend, of having seen and chosen, the air of achieved possession of those vague qualities and quantities that collectively figured to him as the advantage snatched from lucky chances.

Some very complicated 'processing' of meanings is going on here (see below, pp. 109–13). In this, as in the other passages, modes of expression have been chosen (consciously or not) which exert substantial and diverse influences on the reader's experience as he or she 'decodes', retrieves the meaning from its structure of expression. Briefly, the structure of the syntactic surface has a direct impact on the activity of reading – it may hold the reader up as he progresses left-to-right through a text, or advance his progress smoothly; or alternate these effects, 'punctuating' the text and directing the reader's attention more to some parts of the meaning, less to others. Marked tendencies to repeat the same syntactic types (short or long sentences, sentences with co-ordinated rather than subordinated clauses, verb-less sentences, etc.) give rise to a variety of stylistic impressions: we call a writer's language 'terse', or 'flowing', 'convoluted', 'staccato', 'ponderous' and so on.

More important than these quasi-physical impressions are the influences of surface structure on the reader's apprehension of *rhetorical* facets of a text. What this means is that the manner of expression, as much as the content expressed, allows the reader to construct an image of the author of a text, or rather, not of the author himself, but of the posture he has created for that particular work. In the case of a work of prose fiction, we become conscious of an 'implied author' in command of the language, taking up stances in relation to the literary and ideological traditions within which the book is written, in relation to the content of the book (ideas, characters, narrator if any) and in relation to the implied readership. These complex feature of 'tone', 'point of view', readily discernible to the experienced reader who is familiar with the conventions within which a novel is written, will be a major preoccupation of chapter 4 of this book. In terms of the linguistic theory employed here, features of tone and style are controlled by the relationship between the surface structure and the deep structure of sentences. I think it will be realized that the distinction between these two levels of structure is a version of the established belief that in linguistic communication there are available 'different ways' (surface structures) 'of saying the same thing' (deep structure). This thesis is basic to traditional stylistics as well as to contemporary linguistics.

Paraphrase and ambiguity

The standard demonstrations of the existence of two levels of language, an underlying level of semantic structure as well as the surface structure we observe, appeal to the situations of *paraphrase* (or *synonymy*) and *ambiguity*. Sentences which are superficially dissimilar but 'mean the same' (are synonymous) are said to have the same deep structure. We can see that there is thus no one-to-one relationship between *meaning* and *form*; meaning is constant while form or surface structure diverges:

John broke the window.
The window was broken by John.

In each of the above sentences, 'John' bears exactly the same semantic relationship to the verb 'break' (*agent*); similarly 'the window' has the same relationship to the verb (*object*); and 'John' has the same causative relationship to 'the window'. The same proposition, or the same cognitive content, is conveyed by both of these sentences; yet they differ radically in surface structure. The overt differences (e.g. the *-n* or its absence on 'broke', the presence or absence of 'by') are pure features of surface structure, contributing nothing to *meaning* as I am defining it: cognitive or propositional meaning residing in deep structure. Of course, to say that surface structure features have no semantic function by no means entails that they have no communicative function whatsoever; on the contrary, they are of great significance in stylistic and rhetorical analysis, as we shall see. It is precisely a writer's choice of surface structures from among possible alternatives for expressing his intended deep structures which governs the 'connotations' or 'reverbera- tions' referred to above. Different surface structures make a radical difference to the impression the text makes on the reader: to his sense of the author's tone, of the rhythm of the text, of its affiliations with other texts; above all, to the reader's impression of the place of a text and of its author among the thought-patterns of a culture.

The converse of paraphrase, ambiguity, also shows the need for proposing a separate underlying level of semantic structure only indirectly related to surface structure. A good, if now unoriginal, example is

Flying planes can be dangerous.

which can be understood as either 'It can be dangerous (for someone) to fly planes' or 'planes which fly (or planes in flight) can be dangerous'. The semantic structure of the first meaning includes the proposition 'X (agent) flies planes (object)' whereas the second contains 'Planes (agent) fly'. This doubleness of meaning can be no more inferred from mere observation of the single surface than can single-ness of meaning in the dual surfaces of the synonymous sentences. (The English speaker of course knows the rules for connecting superficial and underlying structures, and when an ambiguous sentence is in context he can retrieve the meanings, despite unstraightforward and unrevealing surface structures.)

Elements of deep structure

The question of what terms and concepts should be used to describe the elements of deep structure is a complicated and controversial one, and I cannot hope to do more than indicate some of the rudiments.

From our point of view, the most important aspects of the deep structure of a sentence are *proposition* and *modality*. The propositional element of the deep structure of a sentence makes reference to some phenomenon or idea outside of language, and attributes some property to it. Thus

The dog barks

picks out, refers to, a category of object in our extra-linguistic experience (dog) and predicates an action of it (barks). The relationship between the noun and the predicate forms the semantic skeleton of the proposition; such relationships (here, agent-action) are of the utmost importance in semantics and in narrative analysis, and I will have more to say about them shortly.

Modality covers all those features of discourse which concern a speaker's or writer's attitude to, or commitment to, the value or applicability of the propositional content of an utterance, and concomitantly, his relationship with whoever he directs the speech act to. This particular example-sentence happens to be modally ambiguous. A speaker might utter it in the performance of one of several distinct speech acts: (*a*) to claim, as a general truth, that it is a characteristic of all dogs that they bark (cf. 'The dog is a carnivore'); (*b*) to state, as a particular comment, that some individual dog is in the habit of barking (cf. 'Rover barks at 6 p.m. every evening'); (*c*) to describe, narratively, an ongoing act of barking (cf. 'The burglar approaches the window; the dog barks; the burglar is startled and runs away'). Other contrasts of modality, easier to grasp, include question ('Is the dog barking?'), assertion ('The dog *does* bark'), command ('Bark, you wretched dog!'), negation ('The dog isn't barking'). These are all different speech acts attaching different modalities to what is basically the same proposition, and evidently they differ in the speaker's attitude to his material and/or his relationship with his interlocutor. Modality relates directly to point of view in fiction; see chapter 4.

The analysis of the *propositional* part of deep structure is of great interest: it is the core of cognitive content on which the whole meaning is built. The semantic nucleus of a proposition is a '*predicate*', often realized as a verb or an adjective in surface structure: 'break', 'shut', 'climb', 'speak', 'laugh', 'believe', 'widen', 'tall', 'sad', 'wide', 'sleepy', 'noisy', 'square', etc. Predicates fall into a number of basic semantic types which seem, interestingly, to answer closely to some fundamental distinctions in the ways human beings perceive properties, action and change in the phenomenal world: some are *actions* ('climb', 'run', 'laugh', 'shout'), some are *states* ('believe', 'hear', 'know', 'tall', 'sad', 'wide'), some are *changes of state* ('break', 'shut', 'widen'). It is possible that this semantic classification may derive from innate categories of essential human perception, and so it may be universal; but this speculation need not detain us; sufficient that this is a basic semantic classification which organizes the deep structure of sentences in the languages with which we will be concerned. You may have noticed that actions and changes of state are generally expressed as verbs in English surface structure, states as adjectives. This is a tendency only: there are many state predicates such as 'know', 'hear', 'see', 'grieve' which are realized as verbs. Nominals in surface structure are often derived from predicates: they conceal a range of underlying predicates of different semantic types: 'brotherhood' (state), 'nationalization' (change of state), 'proclamation' (action). This is yet another example of the obliqueness of the conventions which give rise to non-correspondence of deep and surface structures: a noun in the surface structure, connoting a 'thing'-type concept, has often neutralized the actional force of an underlying predicate. Activities turn into objects *en route* from deep to surface structure.

I called the predicate the 'semantic nucleus' of a proposition. A proposition is completed by attaching a *noun* or nouns to the predicate. If a predicate communicates an event or a state of affairs, the nouns associated with it specify the participants in that event, or the objects in that state. Two correlations between predicates and nouns are of interest. First, choice of predicate determines the *number* of nouns that can be selected to go with it. It may require one noun, or more than one noun, to complete its meaning. A state predicate demands only one, viz. the name of the object in that state: 'Peter is tall', or 'a sad man'.* Action

* In these and the following examples, I have deliberately chosen expressions with a variety of surface structures to show the diversity of possible transformations of propositional structures. These two ex-

predicates similarly require only one noun, that denoting the active participant: 'the children danced', or 'singing-bird'. Change of state predicates may take one accompanying noun ('the window broke'), or two ('John broke the window' or 'a stone broke the window'), or three ('John broke the window with a stone').

The second relationship between predicates and nouns concerns which types of nouns can accompany which types of predicate. Nouns in deep structure are said to play different *roles* (or, to use a more traditional term, to be in different *cases*). When we study the meanings of nouns in simple (one-predicate) sentences which contain several nouns, such as 'John broke the window with a stone', we discover that the different nouns play distinct roles in relation to the predicate, and on further investigation we find that these roles are quite few in total and crop up regularly in other sentences too. 'John' is the animate instigator of an action, and his role could be called *agent*; 'the children' and 'bird' (above) are also agents, but not 'Peter' or 'man' – no action is performed – nor, of course, 'the window' in any of the above sentences where it occurs. 'The window' might be termed *object*: not surface structure object as in traditional grammar, the nominal which follows the verb in many English sentences, but object as a semantic, deep structure role – that which is caused by John's action to come into the state of being broken. A semantic (deep) object may occur in various syntactic (surface) positions, including even the surface subject position, preceding the verb: 'the window broke', 'the book was dropped'. In the earlier examples, 'Peter is tall' and 'a sad man', 'Peter' and 'man' could also be called objects, though some linguists subdivide the category, to distinguish *objects* which simply have external properties predicated of them ('a tall man'), from *experiencers*

---

amples are both 'state predicate + noun' in the deep structure but have been transformed to 'noun + *is* + adjective' and 'adjective + noun' respectively in the surface syntax.

where the predicate mentions a state of mind ('a sad man') or a sensation ('my toe throbbed'), from *patients*, animates who have something done to them ('He was pushed over', 'Bill kicked James'), from *beneficiaries* ('Mary' in 'We sent Mary some flowers') and so on.

Other noun-roles such as *instrument* ('stone' in 'John broke the window with a stone') and *location* ('We visited Helsinki') will be introduced when necessary. The total number is probably quite small. At the moment, it is more important to grasp the principle than to establish the complete set.

Meaning and world-view

There are many aspects of meaning which I have had to neglect – most noticeably, perhaps, those features which distinguish individual words from each other as a dictionary does: 'cat' from 'dog', 'window' from 'stone', etc. Some of these factors will emerge in later chapters; e.g. for word-distinguishing semantic features, see pp. 33–41 below. I have chosen to concentrate on some of the most abstract but most powerful elements of meaning. Recall some of the terms used: action, state, change of state, agent, object, patient, instrument, location. These semantic categories are, I think, pretty close to the structures which we human beings employ to make sense of the world we live in – at least, human beings in the European or Europeanized cultures whose narrative literature I will sample. Perhaps other cultures look at the world in quite different ways: perhaps, specifically, cultures which have languages structured very differently from English, French, German, Russian, Latin, etc. At any rate, I and my readers live in a world which we represent to ourselves as containing a multiplicity of separate things situated at identifiable points in space and time; some of these entities are capable of initiating actions and change by willed or unconscious drive, whereas others lack this faculty of responsibility, this power to cause the world to change: animacy versus inanimacy is one of our basic conceptual distinctions, and we show our respect for this dichotomy by growing anxious about phenomena which behave on the borderline: thunder, electricity, ghosts, gods. Of course, the above notions depend on a prior distinction which we feel it is natural to make, between things on the one hand and attributes on the other; between attributes such as movement or change, versus stability. We distinguish concrete from abstract, opposites from equivalents, and so on. All of these cognitive or logical distinctions are expressed in the deep structure of sentences, and all of them figure in our ways of thinking about fictional structure.

In general, then, talk about 'world-view', about an individual's, or a society's, or a novel's, modes of representation of reality, is highly compatible, in terms of what seem the most natural analytic notions, with talk about the deep structure of sentences. Language and the inner representation of outer reality are intimately interconnected, and we can notice and be impressed with this without getting into a chicken-and-egg dilemma about which influences which. The connection of language and world-view, and the availability, through linguistics, of a theory and a descriptive method for handling this connection, have some very notable implications for the study of fiction. Three applications of this theory may be mentioned briefly, and they will be developed later in the book: (a) characters and incidents in fiction may closely resemble the stock of predicate-types and noun-types; (b) within the sentence, a writer's preference for or avoidance of certain types of deep structure may signify particular cognitive tendencies; (c) a writer may *transform* his deep structures into surface structures which radically modify our apprehension of the propositional meaning of the text: agents may vanish, action may yield place to stasis, objects may take on strange human-like forces and volitions.

Transformations

The invention of the concept of *transformation*, twenty years ago, revolutionized linguistic theory. Adapting an idea of his teacher, Zellig Harris, Noam Chomsky developed an analytic device which vastly increased the power of grammars to explain sentence structure and the overall design of languages. Basically, the idea of transformation is a simple one, but its application to syntactic description is complex and technical, and has been subject to controversy and redefinition over the years, while still remaining accepted as the central technique in syntactic description.

In this context, I cannot do more than describe transformations in the most informal terms, which will hardly satisfy the experts. So I strongly urge readers to consult one of the introductory books on transformational grammar cited in the bibliography; if possible, also to read Chomsky's first book, *Syntactic Structures*, carefully, working through the details of his examples with pencil and paper.

Transformations can be thought about in several different ways; I will mention two, both of them close to the technical definition; there are other, somewhat metaphoric, usages, harmless if used with caution and valuable in practical criticism.

First, transformations define the relationship between deep (semantic) and superficial (syntactic) structures in a given sentence. A predicate–noun–modality cluster of meanings is an *abstract* entity which is to be absolutely distinguished from the ordered sequence of symbols, ultimately written characters or vocal sounds, which are used to express it. Transformations are formal operations which convert abstract meaning into surface structure by an ordered series of structural changes. For example, suppose we have a simple propositional structure

action, agent

where the action predicate is to be 'run' and the agent the noun 'John'. In English the rule is that, when there is only one noun in a sentence, it goes to the left of the verb. So a transformation repositions the agent, thus

action, agent $\longrightarrow$ agent + action

The transformation thus lays the basis of spatio-temporal order: 'John' precedes 'runs'. Other transformations ensure that the structure is finally realized as 'John runs': including (for instance) operations to ensure that no definite article occurs before the proper noun 'John'; to realize present tense as an '-s' attached to the verb; to ensure that this '-s' is pronounced [z] rather than [s] (contrast [s] in 'hits'). These operations which supply and rearrange structure will be correspondingly more complex as the meanings to be expressed are more complicated. I will have to rely on my readers to study and digest more interesting examples in the textbooks.

In the above characterization, transformations are regarded as 'realization rules', rules for deriving surface structures – space-time structures – from underlying abstract meanings. A second perspective is to see them as rules for relating sentences one to another. For instance, it is a standard observation of transformational grammarians that *active* and *passive* sentences are closely related to one another: 'John broke the window' / 'The window was broken by John'. The close similarity can be seen in the fact that, if either of these sentences is true, the other one is necessarily true; and there must be some linguistic explanation for this fact. For a start, they have the same propositional content, the same predicate and noun-roles:

change-of-state, object, agent

One series of transformations derives the passive by placing the object to the left of the verb, the agent phrase 'by John' to its right, and arranging the correct morphology for the verb and its auxiliary, resulting in the passive 'the window was broken by John'. An alternative set of transformations disposes the nouns at opposite ends of the sentence, and deletes the preposition 'by' (which is the natural marker of the agent case in English): so we have the active form 'John broke the window'. The relationship between the two sentences can be expressed as the relationship between the two sets of transformational rules for realizing one semantic structure in two distinct ways.

Relationships between other ranges of sentence-constructions can be informatively treated in a similar way. For instance, many sentences containing adjectives have counterparts with relative clauses:

(*a*) The hungry guest ate all the olives.
(*b*) The guest, who was hungry, ate all the olives.

A transformational description can handle this relationship by giving both sentences a common sequence of derivational rules up to a certain point: i.e. deriving (*a*) in a series of steps which would first derive (*b*) (both having the same deep structure on which the transformations operate, because both have the same meaning), then reducing the relative clause to the adjective 'hungry', and finally repositioning the adjective before the noun 'guest'. (The transformational 'history' of this pair of constructions is detailed in most of the handbooks.)

Transformations and perspective

The cognitive patterns I have been discussing relate to language at the level of deep structure; but they are presented to a reader through the level of surface structure, and, as we have seen, surface syntax is only an indirect expression of underlying semantic organization. Arranging the shape of his linguistic surface, a writer enjoys wide choices in manner

of expression. The choices* he makes, his favoured transformations, powerfully affect *perspective* upon meaning, by
directing our attention on the content and the structure of
the depicted world of a fiction in one way or another.

Consider again the active/passive pair (1) 'John broke
the window' (2) 'The window was broken by John.' These
sentences are distinct transformational realizations of the
same semantic structure, a semantic base which in turn
refers to the same event. The implications of the two descriptions differ. In the first sentence, the focus is on John and
the action of breaking; in the second, the window and its
change of state are emphasized, the agent subordinated.
(2) assumes that we are talking about John and goes on to
tell us something new about him, whereas (3) is an utterance on the given topic of the window, while the information
that it was John who broke it is new. The passive transformation also allows us to omit mention of the agent altogether:
(3) 'The window was broken.' Conceptually, a *cause* is
implicit: it doesn't make sense to say 'The window was
broken but it wasn't broken by anything.' But a writer may
consistently exercise the option not to mention the agent and
so give the impression of a world in which things happen
without any evident cause, or a world in which the power
of the human will to influence the course of things is apparently diminished. Conversely, the exercise of the will to
act may be emphasized by the use of transformations which
preserve the direct expression of active (and even more,
active transitive) structures – as we saw in 'Maggie suddenly
rushed out . . . and dipped her head in a basin of water'
(pp. 8–9 above).

The passage from *The Mill on the Floss* provides another
example of the perspective significance of transformations.
The nouns 'disappointment' and 'determination' are trans-

---

* 'Choice' and 'favour' are not necessarily conscious; a writer's constructions may betray his patterns of thought without his intending
that they do so.

formations of predicates – George Eliot could have written 'Maggie was disappointed', 'Maggie was determined'. This transformational process, a very common one in European languages, is called *nominalization*. We shall meet this transformation, the expression of a deep structure predicate as a surface structure nominal, frequently in our descriptive studies (see, e.g., pp. 111–13 below): it has remarkably flexible stylistic potential, producing a number of quite distinct slantings of underlying meaning. In the present case, the effect is to objectify or reify Maggie's feelings, to endow them with a sense of concrete presence, foregrounding them in the reader's as in Maggie's experience like sharp-outlined objects in the foreground of a painting. Now feelings ('states' in linguistic terms) are not objects, of course, so when the novelist chooses to refer to them in a syntax associated with objects, she is directing our view of this part of the cognitive world of the novel in quite a special way. This effect of nominalization on cognitive reorientation is additional to and distinct from its purely surface-structural consequence of producing long words like 'disappointment' which are prominent through weighty syllabic structure, as noted above.

It could well be that, when we discuss meaning and structure in novels, the transformational dimension is the one which merits our closest attention. Our only access to the underlying meanings of texts is via the orders, forms and choices of words which we encounter on the surface, that is to say, we experience meaning only in the form given by the realization rules, the transformations, which the text employs. Meaning always comes to us processed by the form in which it is expressed. This is the theme of my main chapter, 4, in which I show how the content of fiction is constantly interpreted by the expressive conventions of the discourse of the novel.

Speculative extensions

I suggested that the deep structure of the sentence codes our experiences in categories (agent, state, etc.) conveniently appropriate to the way we naturally conceive of the world; transformations add a perspective to this coding, sometimes fundamentally altering the presentation of the semantic structure. Novels, like sentences, are codings of experience, and there is good reason to believe that their basic structural categories have a lot in common with the elements of sentence structure.

Single sentences might be thought of as mini-narratives: 'John broke the window' records an event, coding it as an Agent + Change-of-state + Object semantic structure of one predicate and two nouns; the sentence could also serve as a *précis* or synopsis of a much longer narrative, a recapitulation of the combined force of the literal predicates and nouns of a sequence of many sentences. That a sequence of sentences (a whole text) has the same semantic structure as a single sentence is suggested by the availability of acceptable one-sentence paraphrases. A sentence which sums the action of a large segment of Dostoevsky's *Crime and Punishment* (1865–6) is 'Raskolnikov killed the old woman'; for Joyce's *A Portrait of the Artist as a Young Man* (1916) 'Stephen grew up in circumstances which persuaded him that he must free himself artistically by rejecting his religion, his family and his country'; Dickens's *David Copperfield* (1850) 'After false goals and an unwise marriage, David achieved fame as a writer and marital happiness'; and so on.

Note that synopsis-sentences, as well as capturing semantic roles patently relevant to the content-structures of the novels, also in their structural order of clauses and phrases reflect temporal and causal sequence. The problem of which might be the best of competing paraphrases need not detain us. We need to note only that narratives are manifestly reducible to sentence-brief synopses, and the reason why this is so should already be clear: sentences and narratives are equally man-made constructions of reality, and the constructional principles are the same. People (at least in the same culture) organize their experience of the world in common ways, and the patterns they rely upon are the same for tales which take many hours in the reading as for the minimal units of linguistic communication, sentences, which although brief are no less complete narratively and conceptually.

The theory and methods for describing sentences are by now well advanced; the theory and criticism of narrative somewhat less so. If the structure of narrative corresponds to that of sentences, then the criticism of fiction may profit from the application of linguistic concepts to the broader structural patterns of novels.

The plausibility of such application may be suggested by some informal examples. Picaresque novels, such as Henry Fielding's *Tom Jones* (1749) or John Barth's *The Sot-Weed Factor* (1960) are structured on a hectic series of narrative 'predicates' beginning with an initial change of state from stability to disorder. Squire Allworthy returns from London to find an infant bastard asleep in his bed: an astonishing modification of his hitherto settled state of life. The child, Tom Jones, grown up, leaves home and embarks successively on a thick-and-fast series of hazardous 'action verbs' (or is the 'patient' in respect of actions initiated by agents other than himself) precipitating him through a quest across England which only after 800 pages of encounters with a bewildering succession of 'nouns' of many 'roles' brings him to a 'state' of equilibrium comparable to his peaceful origin. A modern picaresque, *Ulysses*, retains the scrambling sequence of change-of-state predicates, but adds an indulgence in state predicates attached to Leopold and Molly Bloom and to Stephen. A Virginia Woolf or a Henry James novel dwells on states to the subordination of actions. In narrative literature generally, analogues for the noun roles are easily found: Fanny Price in Jane Austen's *Mansfield Park* (1814) is a heroine cast in the ironically reiterated role of 'patient'; Gatsby in Scott Fitzgerald's novel (1925) is 'agent', grand manipulator in a quest for his personal romantic ends, but terminates as 'patient'. Pandarus in the various versions of the Troilus and Cressida legend is ambiguously 'agent' or 'instrument'.

I think the structural analogy between sentence and narrative text will already be clear. As a basis for analysis, this analogy has been used in the work of the French structuralists, particularly that of A-J. Greimas and of Tzvetan Todorov.* The categories of linguistic structure have also been interestingly applied to communication in other media – to fashion, architecture, popular culture by Roland Barthes, to cinema by Christian Metz. I will have a little more to say about language structure and narrative structure in the next chapter, and then for the remainder of this book will return from this analogy of sentence-structure and text-structure to language proper: to a study of some implications of the structure of actual sentences for the character of the texts built out of them.

* See Terence Hawkes, *Structuralism and Semiotics*.

2 ELEMENTS

Elements of the text in traditional poetics

EVER since classical times, students of literature have speculated on the 'parts' or 'elements' or 'components' of literary works. Literary texts are commonly regarded as objects, things, artefacts, having a similar objective status to the organic and inorganic entities which fill our world. But when we represent literary works as 'objects', we are not thinking of the physical *books* which contain or record them: the work itself is an abstract entity, the book is only the physical medium through which it is made accessible to the consumer. (But some works, e.g. Sterne's *Tristam Shandy* (1759-67) to some extent, Christine Brooke-Rose's *Thru* (1975) almost totally, highlight the physical medium by typographical games more characteristic of concrete poetry than the novel.)

The literary work being an abstraction, we need a 'model' to represent its features to ourselves: we have to think about its elements in terms of some other, but relevant, object which we know better or can perceive more directly. We apply a metaphor to the text-object we are trying to understand – we might, for instance, picture the text as if it were a machine with its various parts all working in integration, or as an animal with its distinct life-organs functioning in their diverse but inter-related ways, or as a plant with its delicate processes of bio-chemical synthesis. Organic models of literary structure have been especially popular since the Romantic period.

Way back in Greek antiquity, Aristotle invited his students to consider the literary work as if it were an animal, with its well-formed proportions, its parts appropriate to its function in the world. But when Aristotle actually came to list the parts of the type of poem with which he was most concerned, the tragic drama, he abandoned this metaphor, and sketched out the model which has been most popular and influential in subsequent literary theory: he pictured the drama as a kind of microcosmic representation of human society. For Aristotle, the parts of the drama are as follows: action, character, diction, spectacle, music, thought. Literature is for Aristotle a mode of imitation, a representation of the world, so his parts of the literary work correspond to various major elements which the human being recognizes in his intuitive engagement with the world: the separate identity of persons, their use of language, their thoughts, the succession of events and actions through time, the sights that are seen and the sounds that are heard. These elements, then, resemble the categories of thought and perception which I mentioned in the previous chapter, and are possibly susceptible to formal explanation by applying the analogy of categories of sentence-structure, as previously suggested.

Innumerable adaptations of the Aristotelian scheme have been proposed. There have been some attempts, principally by critics at the University of Chicago, to set up formal systems of elements for literary genres which Aristotle could not have known, including the novel, but these have been unconvincing because they have lacked a relevant 'model'. Informally, Aristotle's components or similar ones have passed naturally into common parlance about novels. Among such terms, the following seem to be indispensable, and also suitable for explication through our linguistic model: *language* (or *style*), *plot, character, setting, theme*. There are scores of vague secondary terms, some of which – e.g. *structure* and *texture* – do a lot of work in critical writing but which can only be stabilized after the major elements have been assembled into a coherent frame. In the next section we will refer to the components of sentences to provide a model for the elements of texts.

Elements of text grammar

The frame for sentences, from which we will draw our analogy, may be displayed as follows:

a **sentence** has a **surface structure**
formed by **transformations** of a
semantic deep structure consisting of a
modality component plus a **propositional** component
the latter based on a
predicate attended by one or more **nouns**
in different **roles**

Some applications of this scheme to narrative texts are very easily made. The surface structure of a text (which is a sequence of sentences) has, like the surface structure of a sentence, qualities such as sequence, rhythm, spatial and temporal expressiveness of various kinds: pagination, paragraphing, chapter- and other section-divisions; variations of typography, wherever the novelist has dictated such. Textual surface structure also includes many features traditionally associated with the idea of 'style', particularly those features depending on the rhythm of sentences and of their arrangements in sequences. *Transformations* form textual, like sentential, surface structures out of the chosen abstract elements beneath the surface.

Textual deep structure: narrative predicates and nouns

The submarine elements which are less visible in the text (plot, character, theme), and in which critics are most interested, display a remarkable correspondence with the underlying components of the semantic deep structure of sentences. The plot of a narrative text may be thought of as a sequence of verbs or predicates, each one establishing a state, an action, a change of state in the participants: when we précis a story we report this sequence: e.g. 'X was born', 'X met Y', 'X embarked on a career', 'Y observed X', 'X forgot Y', 'Y tracked X down', 'X got into difficulties', 'Y rescued X' etc. If this sounds trivial, it is because I have given the example predicates rather general meanings – and deliberately so. Many novelists have discovered that there is a limited number of plots available, and that all have already been written. Just as verbs in sentences reduce to a small number of elemental types, so narrative predicates may fall into a set of basic primitives which define the range of actional possibilities for human beings and for other objects.

This theory that narrative plots reduce to arrangements of stock 'verbs' from a finite set of possibilities has been developed by the French structuralists on the basis of analyses of Russian folk-tales undertaken in the 1920s by Vladimir Propp.* Propp works with classifications of both verbs and nouns. His nouns, or 'dramatis personae' as he calls them, are *hero, dispatcher, villain, helper, donor, sought-for-person, false hero*. The verbs, for the Russian tales, are thirty-one 'functions of the dramatis personae', e.g. *absentation, reconnaissance, trickery, departure, provision or receipt of a magical agent, pursuit*, etc. Some of these narrative predicates are doubtless specific to the genre Propp analyses; lists for other conventionalized genres can be easily thought up (detective fiction, novels of emotional development or 'sentimental education', Gothic fiction, women's romantic literature, spy

* Cf. Terence Hawkes, *Structuralism and Semiotics* pp. 67–9 and 91–5.

stories, voyages of discovery, etc., each have their standard suite of narrative predicates, stock 'verbs' which advance the plot or designate its stages). Some predicates like *pursuit, quest, murder, captivity, rejection, flight,* which can be expressed in very general terms, must have wide application to many superficially different types of narrative.

The nouns in the deep structure of fiction (mostly characters, but not only) can be classified into roles such as 'agent', 'patient', 'beneficiary', 'intermediary', 'goal', 'location' and the like. It must be admitted at once that such analysis, examples of which may be found in the work of French critics and theoreticians such as Todorov and Greimas, is extremely schematic, reducing stories and their participants to formulae and ciphers. The object of analysis, at this extreme level of abstraction, is to show that narratives draw from a common pool of basic schemes, just as (and on the same principles as) all sentences express a small universal range of deep semantic structures.

A less reductive, less universalizing, approach is needed in practical criticism. In more pragmatic descriptive criticism, we need to specify and subdivide the predicates and nouns according to the conventional structures relevant to particular types and periods in the history of narrative fiction. The role 'agent', for instance, covers a range of character-types who in different ways initiate sequences of actions, manipulate other characters, change or definitively resolve the order of the plot. Tom Jones, Billy Liar, Lucky Jim, Holden Caulfield (*The Catcher in the Rye*), Gulley Jimson (*The Horse's Mouth*), precipitate the plot constantly from stage to stage, but usually by some almost accidental action not entirely within their responsibility or will. By contrast, Bulstrode in *Middlemarch*, Fagin in *Oliver Twist*, Murdstone in *David Copperfield*, Tom Buchanan in *The Great Gatsby*, Al and Max in *The Killers*, Jason Compson in *The Sound and the Fury* manipulate the action by design, but often indirectly, often using other characters as 'instruments'

(Sykes, Miss Murdstone, Jason's mother, etc.). These are clearly quite distinct types of 'agent', and it might be profitable to distinguish them in terms of their typical relationships with narrative predicates rather than in terms of intrinsic psychological or moral features. So, for example, the distinction between 'rogues' and 'villains' may be seen as a deep grammatical distinction: a rogue is not always in control of his actions – he is often manipulated as instrument or patient; a villain is definitely agent, but often covertly so, working through an instrument, and always a persecutor of patients.

Typical and individual

This 'actantial' or 'functional' theory of characters and their relationships to narrative predicates needs a lot more development before it can provide solid reference points in criticism and novel theory. If we can imagine it developed, we may still see a potential defect: its aim is to devise, with the authority of linguistic theory, a set of types of narrative situation and of participants in stories, whereas (it might be said) the goal, and central aesthetic, of the novel is to express particularity, specificity, individuality.

Actually, the correctness of this claim about individuality is questionable; the distinction between 'type' and 'individual' as subjects of fiction is historical rather than absolute. Oral folk-narrative, myth and early European written tales (Chaucer, Boccaccio, Marguerite de Navarre), even down to the works of Balzac, are preoccupied with (or contented with, if you like) the typical in human behaviour. The assumptions of medieval and Renaissance psychology, physiology and sociology made it seem natural for early fiction to present the protagonists in narrative as having the attributes of some pre-defined category. (Note that Propp, Todorov, Barthes and Lévi-Strauss have tended to take classical, traditional, oral materials for their examples; and that the 'actantial' model of character stems from their writings and those of their colleagues.) In the nineteenth century, novelists such as Flaubert, George Eliot, Dostoevsky consolidated a much more individual-oriented fiction, a tradition culminating in the intense exploration of personality and inner consciousness in the work of Henry James, Proust, Joyce, Virginia Woolf. This psychological/ spiritual tradition is attended by an increasing fascination with physical details of person and place, and a growing minuteness in recording them. Both trends can be related to massive changes in scientific thought (empiricism in biology, psychology, etc.) and in technology (e.g. photography) and to the ethic of personal opportunism to which the emergent bourgeoisie was devoted. It is these powerful – but strictly historical and relative – intellectual and social changes which have led many critics of fiction to believe that novels have a strong concern with the idiosyncratic in person and place. How can linguistics cater for this preoccupation with the individual?

It can't and shouldn't pretend to account for individuality. It can, however, suggest ways of adding to 'character' more concrete qualities than its basic actantial model provides. Character-individuality in fiction is an illusion, a projection onto texts of the cultured expectations of the community of modern novel-readers. Anything which is mediated through a social communication system is conventional; the 'people' of fiction are transmitted through the conventions of fiction-language. (As popular social theorists such as Erving Goffman and Umberto Eco have argued, each biological person [outside fiction, you and I etc.] is also made up of public signs voiced in lots of socio-cultural 'languages'.) Certainly, there is more differentiated substance about them than their actantial roles as agent, beneficiary, etc., but this substance is conventional. To understand how the characters of fiction acquire their impression of substance, we may find it helpful to compare them with nouns in ordinary language. We will see that the meanings of the latter are built out of conventional semantic materials belonging not to themselves but to the vocabulary as a whole. It is quite likely that the illusion of 'character' is created in a parallel way.

Nouns and 'characters': semantic analysis

So far I have discussed nouns only from the point of view of their roles in the structure of propositions, and extended this role-analysis to the functions of the *dramatis personae* in plot-construction. As far as roles or cases in language or narrative are concerned, individual differences of word-meaning are more or less immaterial (with the exception of some general restrictions, e.g. predicates like 'laugh' must have animate subjects). Role-structure is the same whether one says 'The boy laughed' or 'The girl laughed' (but 'The stone laughed' is ungrammatical). And Propp has shown that there are marked differences among *dramatis personae* which have no effect on narrative structure. To quote from an example of his:

(a) The king sends Ivan to find the princess. Ivan leaves.
(b) The blacksmith sends his apprentice to find the cow. The apprentice leaves.

are functionally equivalent as narrative schemes, in all their terms. The difference between the king and the blacksmith, like that between 'the boy' and 'the girl' in sentence-structure, is important at a different level, and is accounted for at a different level of analysis.

We now consider nouns not as functions but as *lexical items*, that is, as parts of the vocabulary, as they might be listed in a dictionary, not elements in propositional or syntactic structure. We suppose that lexical items are distinguished from one another by inherent features of meaning which determine what objects they may be used to refer to.

One proposal for describing these features of meaning goes under the rather forbidding name of *componential analysis.**
Each lexical item is regarded as a set or cluster of components called *distinctive features* or *semantic features* or *semes*.
Words are distinguished according to what features they possess, and, for each feature, the *value* (plus or minus) of that feature. For example, the words 'boy' and 'girl' may be given the following feature analysis:

boy	girl
+CONCRETE	+CONCRETE
+ORGANIC	+ORGANIC
+ANIMATE	+ANIMATE
+HUMAN	+HUMAN
−ADULT	−ADULT
+MALE	−MALE
−FEMALE	+FEMALE

The two words are contrasted only in the values of the final features MALE and FEMALE. This surely captures our intuition that the words have very similar meanings, but are subject to one radical distinction, that of sex. If we compare these lexical items with some others, we can see how componential analysis works. Abstract words like 'fidelity' or 'beauty' must be −CONCRETE, and so features such as ORGANIC, ADULT are irrelevant since they can inhere only in words relating to objects which have physical substance. 'Stone' is −ORGANIC, and therefore of necessity neither +ANIMATE nor −ANIMATE. 'Dog' is −HUMAN, but the features ADULT and MALE are still relevant, because the word can apply to animals that may be young or old, male or female. If we studied more lexical items, we would find ourselves having to postulate new semantic features, of

* See Fowler, *Understanding Language*, ch. 3; Lyons, *Introduction to Theoretical Linguistics*, ch. 10.

course, but we would observe that the new features fitted into one overall network of contrasts and other systematic logical relationships.

The semantic possibilities of a language may be thought of as given by the system of semantic features or 'semes' – some universal but most of them specific to the community concerned – out of which the meanings of words are constructed, and by which words are related and contrasted. The existence of the semantic system explains how it is possible for new lexical items to be created and understood: namely, by reference to and rearrangement of the structures of meaning already encoded in the language. The *system*, repository of the community's verbalized knowledge about the world, is logically prior to, and more important than, the individual lexical item, which is no more than an agreed form attaching to a selected cluster of semes, by convention applicable in speech to a class of objects or ideas.

So also 'character' in fiction: the novelist and his readers make reference to a stock of physical, behavioural, psychological and verbal attributes out of which fictional characters may be put together in somewhat the same way as the police assemble an 'identikit' picture out of a set of pictures of segments of different kinds of faces. In modern 'realistic' fiction, the semes tend to reflect the clichés and stereotypes in terms of which the society which supports the literature sees itself: aggression, materialism, possessiveness, piety, innocence, naïveté, ambition, sensitivity, physical power, femininity, introversion, elegance, verbal wit, rationalism, status, alienation, etc., etc. Needless to say, my list is only a list of guesses, for informal illustrative purposes; no one has yet formalized the theory of characterological semes (Roland Barthes uses the method informally but suggestively in his book S/Z). But the model for the theory – distinctive features – is well established in linguistics, both in phonology and semantics, and the content and names for the semes might well be drawn from sources such as role theory in modern social psychology (cf. Goffman) as well as from a more systematic interpretation of the descriptions which literary critics, reviewers and ordinary readers have assigned to characters in fiction.

As as example of the attachment of semes to a character, consider Tom Buchanan in *The Great Gatsby*. Among the semantic features which constitute him are: restlessness, physical strength, virility, athleticism (both competitive and social), dandyism, wealth, materialism, extravagance, vulgarity, possessiveness, jealousy, untrustworthiness, selfishness, carelessness, cruelty, physical violence, aggression, arrogance, cynicism, contemptuousness, insolence, fractiousness, prejudice, shallowness. Many of these features are explicitly stated, or implied, in the two pages very early in the novel which introduce Tom: *restlessness* – 'drifted here and there unrestfully', 'I felt that Tom would drift on forever seeking, a little wistfully, for the dramatic turbulence of some irrecoverable football game', 'restlessly'; *athleticism* – 'physical accomplishments', 'powerful', 'football', 'played polo', 'football game', 'riding clothes', 'enormous power of that body', 'a great pack of muscle', and so on. Incident and phrase amplify and dramatize these semes as the novel progresses, picking out and highlighting what Nick sees as the crucial ones as he moves towards a judgement on Tom.

A character is, then: (*a*) an 'actant' – s/he performs a role or roles in the structure of the plot; (*b*) an assemblage of semes; (*c*) a proper name – which is a sort of peg on which the attributes (*a*) and (*b*) are hung. Both (*a*) and (*b*) are conventional rather than idiosyncratic. Much of the illusion of individuality may in fact be given by eccentricity or memorizability of the names which a novelist attaches to his more or less conventional figures: Dickens's naming practice is spectacularly efficient in this way, inventing names which are grotesquely distinctive yet often encapsulate some typical actantial or semantic aspect of the character – Gradgrind, Bounderby, Sleary (*Hard Times*,

1854), Snagsby, Dedlock, Jellyby (*Bleak House*, 1853), Wegg, Boffin, Podsnap (*Our Mutual Friend*, 1865), Steerforth, Micawber, Peggotty, Creakle (*David Copperfield*, 1849–50). The power of names to evoke associations is magnificently illustrated by the fantastic two-page list of visitors to Gatsby's house which Nick Carraway reproduces at the beginning of chapter IV of *The Great Gatsby*.

Finally, (*d*), a character is distinguished by the structure and the semantic content of the language and thoughts that are assigned to him. I will be discussing this aspect of characterization in chapter 4, 'Discourse', but must say at once that the representation of speech and thought, like the characterological semes, is to a large degree conventionalized. As far as 'individuality' is concerned, the effect is achieved very often by the most trivial linguistic means: by catch-phrases of the 'I will never desert Mr Micawber' type, or by mannerisms such as the bumbling repetitiousness, the vague 'that sort of thing' of Mr Brooke's speech in *Middlemarch*, by Mithter Thleary's lithp. These isolated verbal particularities are like idiosyncracies of gesture or dress: trivial in themselves, they work once and once only; whoever keeps his hand thrust into the buttoning of his waistcoat is obviously a copy of Napoleon; and being a manifest copy is not a very interesting or enriching mode of fictional existence.

There is more to be said about semes. As a technique for the analysis of the substance of 'character', these conventional features have the advantage that they allow us to connect the properties of a particular fictional persona with other semantic aspects of the work in which he figures: with other characters, with settings, and with thematic content.

It is, remember, the set or *configuration* of features which defines Tom Buchanan; any or all of the constituent features may occur in some other semantic cluster, since no one of them is his unique property. So Tom 'overlaps' with Jordan Baker in respect to some semes (athleticism, competitiveness, hardness), with Daisy in other respects (handsomeness, selfishness, restlessness). The three of them share some semes with Gatsby (wealth, ostentation, selfishness) but are polarized from him by others (Gatsby's romantic idealism). Gatsby's 'extraordinary gift for hope, a romantic readiness', the constantly reiterated foundation of Nick's approval of the hero, sets him apart from the other major protagonists in the novel. The semes 'idealism, romanticism, purposeful-ness' excuse his materialism and criminality; the Buchanan set and the Wilsons, dissimilar in most other attributes, are all distinguished from Gatsby by a pointed lack of any seme of spirituality like the idealism which Nick attributes* to Gatsby; they are all classified as purposeless, hopeless, spiritually dead. The semes, then, because un-idiosyncratic, can serve as the basis for the categorization of characters and the diagramming of their immanent patterns of relationship.

Semantic features in 'settings' and 'themes'

Semantic analysis can be extended to areas of the content of literary works other than 'character' – and in one work, or one genre, *the same semantic features are relevant in the analysis of different structural elements*. Locations, particularly, are formed out of semes which relate significantly, either by equivalence or by contrast, to the meanings of the characters who inhabit them. For instance, moral, psychological and allegorical literature has always emphasized the semantic interdependence of person and place. Dickens provides many examples. In *Hard Times*, Gradgrind's and Bounder-by's houses are architectural diagrams of their semantic make-up; and the physical ambience of Coketown expresses

---

* The semes which categorize all these people are filtered through Nick's discourse, and Nick is an unreliable narrator. A more extended dis-cussion would take account of the extreme ambivalence of Nick's moral relationship to the other characters, and to the implied voice of Scott Fitzgerald.

the oppressed drudgery of the lives of the 'hands'. The chronicler of Michel Butor's *L'emploi du temps* (1957; English translation *Passing Time*, 1961), which is atmospherically strongly reminiscent of *Hard Times*, perceives the inhabitants of Bleston through a semantic grid, which is defined by the properties of the weather, the characteristics of the streets and public buildings, and which is schematized in a street-map printed in the book. The Bower of Bliss in Spenser's *Faerie Queene* (1590–6) is a forerunner of Gatsby's gorgeous palace and his parties.

Physical aspects, and actional details, are a public expression of a selected part of the character's semantic structure. The Buchanans' lavish property on East Egg is used by Tom – and in the re-telling by Nick – as an embodiment of their material existence. Nick's 'weatherbeaten cardboard bungalow', symbolically placed next-door to Gatsby's mansion, is characterized by the semes of modesty, poverty and unobtrusiveness which he wants us to attribute to himself. Myrtle's sordid apartment, maintained by Tom, expresses the vicious, vulgar and violent elements of his character, revealed in his own home only by the occasional gesture.

The semantic interdependence of person and place is most obviously illustrated by the famous 'valley of ashes' between West Egg and New York, home of the Wilsons, menacingly watched over by the eyes of Doctor T. J. Eckleburg:

About half way between West Egg and New York the motor road hastily joins the railroad and runs beside it for a quarter of a mile, so as to shrink away from a certain desolate area of land. This is a valley of ashes – a fantastic farm where ashes grow like wheat into ridges and hills and grotesque gardens; where ashes take the forms of houses and chimneys and rising smoke and, finally, with a transcendent effort, of ash-gray men who move dimly and already crumbling through the powdery air. Occasionally a line of gray cars crawls along an invisible track, gives out a ghastly creak, and comes to rest, and immediately the ash-gray men swarm up with leaden spades and stir up an impenetrable cloud, which screens their obscure operations from your sight.

But above the gray land and the spasms of bleak dust which drift endlessly over it, you perceive, after a moment, the eyes of Doctor T. J. Eckleburg. The eyes of Doctor T. J. Eckleburg are blue and gigantic – their retinas are one yard high. They look out of no face, but instead, from a pair of enormous yellow spectacles which pass over a a non-existent nose. Evidently some wild wag of an oculist set them there to fatten his practice in the borough of Queens, and then sank down himself into eternal blindness, or forgot them and moved away. But his eyes, dimmed a little by many paintless days under sun and rain, brood on over the solemn dumping ground.

. . . . .

The interior was unprosperous and bare; the only car visible was the dust-covered wreck of a Ford which crouched in a dim corner. It had occurred to me that this shadow of a garage must be a blind, and that sumptuous and romantic apartments were concealed overhead, when the proprietor himself appeared in the door of an office, wiping his hands on a piece of waste. He was a blond, spiritless man, anæmic, and faintly handsome. When he saw us a damp gleam of hope sprang into his light blue eyes.

. . . . .

'Oh, sure,' agreed Wilson hurriedly, and went toward the little office, mingling immediately with the cement color of the walls. A white ashen dust veiled his dark suit and his pale hair as it veiled everything in the vicinity – except his wife, who moved close to Tom.

The proprietor, Wilson, husband of Tom's mistress, is hardly an *actant* yet, though in this scene of his first intro-duction he begins to assume the role of the manipulated, the put-upon, patient, having no control over the flow of the plot. He is part of the ashen landscape: gray, lifeless, un-fruitful, spiritless. The landscape does not express him (as Tom's house expresses him while remaining subordinate to him); he is just one part of the expressive system constituted primarily by the valley of ashes.

This expressive system engages the reader at a level higher than the semantic substance of 'characters': the first, and definitive, part of the passage quoted above is manifestly intended to set off symbolic reverberations, to form an implicit statement of part of the theme of the book. The ash-gray men, obscurely and purposelessly toiling in an infernal Dantean landscape, and Wilson himself, who is one of their number – his wife walks through him 'as if he were a ghost' – pallidly symbolize the spiritless walking dead, the vacuous sordid human trash of whom Nick becomes gradu-ally aware and whom he places in moral opposition to his Gatsby redeemed by romantic idealism. Tom, Daisy and Jordan drift aimlessly, like the ashes; like the ashes also, they are dead, despite their physical dynamism; they are 'foul dust'. Their drifting East, away from the puritanical Midwest, is representative of the moral rootlessness of the society they inhabit. In Tom's case particularly, passing through the valley of ashes *en route* to his brutal and callous assignations with Myrtle in New York invests him with the semes of dirt and lifelessness which Nick foregrounds in his account of the asheñ waste land. (A perception of the squalid aridity and spiritual vacuity of modern commercial and fashionable society, figured in terms of a man-made desert, is of course also a central symbol in Eliot's almost contem-poraneous poem *The Waste Land*, 1922. The semes which compose a society's current myths tend to migrate from one literary work to another.)

Modality

In this chapter, I have been discussing some ways in which the structural categories usually employed in the description of sentences (chapter 1 and the simplified diagram on p. 28 above) might be applied as models to help clarify and develop the traditional 'elements' which we invoke when we talk about fictional prose narratives; and I have been informally illustrating the 'second-stage' application of these ideas in practical criticism. I have dwelt on semes and semantic analysis in this chapter, because lack of space prevents further development of this branch of analysis in the present book. It remains to discuss the outstanding component, *modality*, and I will do so fairly briefly, since this forms the subject of a whole and long chapter (4).

Every piece of language is implicitly the utterance of a speaker/writer and implicitly addressed to a hearer/reader: a common sense observation, but easily forgotten when dealing with written texts. In fact, this interpersonal dimension of language has been generally neglected, and often deliberately denied, in both criticism and linguistics. Modern critics have insisted that literature is impersonal and objective; they have wanted to deny that literary works are expressive – the utterance of an individual voice – and persuasive – aimed to change the views of behaviour of a certain class of addressee. And modern linguistics has very much concentrated on the information-channelling function of language, its role as a medium for the transmission of meanings, to the neglect of its function as regulator of interpersonal relationships and as medium for attitudes.

But language abounds in constructions which express, or draw attention to, the actions performed and required, the attitudes displayed and desired, by and in the participants in an act of communication. There are explicit manipulatory structures such as imperatives ('Come here!') and questions ('Can you tell me the answer?'). There is the personal pronoun system (I, you, he, etc.) for orienting the message relative to the parties who share in it: 'I told you he would betray you' sorts 'I' and 'you' into one group, addresser and addressee communicating, distances 'he' outside the assumed intimacy of the primary communicative pair; while the act remains uni-directional: I → you. A speaker has many ways of indicating his involvement with any other person whom he mentions. If he says 'She felt sad' he asserts privileged knowledge of a state only the third party, she, can experience; but if he says 'She seemed sad' he is confessing the externality of his opinion, the fact that it is a guess or judgement.

Then there is a range of linguistic constructions signalling the speaker's degree of commitment to the truth of the proposition he utters. There is the matter-of-fact neutral report: 'He walked to the door'; or the speaker may affirm this vigorously, perhaps anticipating or repudiating a denial by his interlocutor: 'He DID walk to the door'. He may qualify his belief in the truth of the proposition, either selecting from the range of 'modal verbs' such as 'may', 'might', 'should', 'will', 'ought to', 'isn't', etc., or by adding a sentence-adverb such as 'probably', 'definitely', 'certainly', 'perhaps', 'apparently'. These 'belief qualifiers' or 'commitment indicators', whether expressed by modal verbs or by adverbs (or by adjectives transformed out of the latter – 'His apparent betrayal . . .') constitute 'modality' in the traditional sense in linguistics, but I have been using this term, in this chapter and the preceding one, in a broader sense: to refer to the linguistics of personal and interpersonal participation in communicative acts; the (implied) speaker's attitude to his propositional material and to his addressee, the kind of speech act he is performing, and where relevant its intended effect on his addressee or audience.

A point to be emphasized is that modal participation in what he writes is just as inevitable for the writer of a fiction as it is for any other person who utters any sentence. What I called 'neutral report' and illustrated by 'He walked to the door' is *not* non-modal: the speaker takes upon himself the responsibility for vouchsafing the factuality of what he reports, and thus modalizes his utterance in a specific way. It is simply an arbitrary fact about English surface syntax that the modality of this speech act isn't explicitly marked by some word like 'may' or DID. Syntactically 'unmarked' modality is still modality, still implies a specific kind of personal involvement in the act of speech.

It is particularly important for us to agree that all language is modalized (despite appearances, in some cases), because opinion about the novel has, in the last hundred years, moved decisively against the intervention of the author in his verbal fictional creation. Gustave Flaubert, in a letter of September 1857, voiced what has become a dogma in the aesthetics of fiction: 'The artist must be in his work as God is in creation, invisible yet all-powerful; we must sense him everywhere but never see him.' Stephen Dedalus's well-known paraphrase of this, in Joyce's *A Portrait of the Artist as a Young Man* (1916), demands even greater objectivity and impersonality by its omission of the clause about sensing the artist everywhere: 'The artist, like the God of creation, remains within or behind or beyond or above his handiwork, invisible, refined out of existence, indifferent, paring his fingernails.' The novelist, it is said, must refrain from showing his own views and values, must conceal the fact that he alone is privy to all the 'secrets' of the plot and its protagonists. Later in this chapter (pp. 52–4) we will examine an example of an intended 'impersonal' authorial stance and conclude that in such styles of writing the God-author does still take up an identifiable modal position. For further general discussion of modality, point of view and the attitudinal relationships between writer, novel and reader, see chapter 4.

Elements and functions

Out of the nine categories of linguistic structure emphasized by bold type on p. 28 above, I have dwelt on three: surface structure, proposition and modality. These originate as aspects of the structure of sentences, and have been applied here as models for the major classes of 'elements' which traditional criticism has posited for prose fictional narrative texts. I think there is some advantage in distinguishing the words we use to talk of elements of textual structure from the linguistic terms attached to the analogous parts of sentence-structure, so I shall make the following terminological substitution:

Sentence	*Prose fiction*
surface structure	text
modality	discourse
proposition	content

Text means textual surface-structure, the most 'perceptible', 'visible', dimension of a work; close to the literary critic's sense of a text as a formal object. For the linguist, textual surface-structure is a series of sentences linked up to form a continuous and cohesive sequence. The stream of sentences implies a definite pace and rhythm of reading, a particular ordering in the presentation of information, a guiding of the reader's attention and a control of his memory. As we will see in the next chapter, there is an intimate and regular connection between the ordering of information and the required 'voice-tune' of a reading, so the relationship between syntax and information is a central topic in textual structure. I will also include other physical aspects of texts under 'textual structure', e.g. typography, paragraphing, etc.

Discourse is studied in all aspects of the novel to which concepts like 'dialogue', 'point of view', 'attitude', 'world-view', 'tone', are relevant: the indication in language structure of the author's beliefs, the character of his thought-processes, the types of judgement he makes; similarly for the narrator and the characters within the fiction; and the whole network of interpersonal relationships between author, characters and implied reader, as these are mediated through language. Discourse in my sense is analogous to modality in the structure of sentences, and is built up by modal verbs ('may', etc.), sentence-adverbs ('possibly'), verbs like 'seem' and 'feel', personal pronouns, acts of speech such as imperative and question, etc.

As for *content* (not the happiest of terms, I know), I mean by this plot, character, setting, theme, regarded in terms of deep verbs, nouns and semantic features, as above. For the reasons given (p. xi), I will offer very little explicit analysis of this dimension of narrative structure, believing that it is my business as a linguist to concentrate more on the sentence-structure of texts. However, since 'form' and 'content' are ultimately inseparable (transformations process meanings), it is natural that some of my comments on linguistic structure will imply views about what is going on beneath the surface, and will thus tend towards interpretation.

In deciding to organize my argument by reference to these three analytic categories, I have been influenced by a linguistic theory outside that of 'transformational grammar': the 'functional' approach of the British linguist M. A. K. Halliday. Whereas the transformational grammarians, like their traditional predecessors, give the impression that language serves *only* to convey propositional meanings, Halliday makes it a first principle that every utterance performs several jobs simultaneously, only one of which could be regarded as propositional. Also, he stresses that the linguist should always appeal to the *function* of an utterance, in its social and interpersonal context, to explain why that utterance manifests its particular structure. He postulates that language structure is ultimately motivated by the contextual functions it is called on to fulfil.

Halliday proposes three concurrent or simultaneous 'functions': *textual, interpersonal* and *ideational*. I have modelled my 'textual structure' quite closely on Halliday's 'textual function'; his 'interpersonal function' provides a way of discussing an important part of my category 'discourse'. The 'ideational function' is an approach to the semantic structure of sentences, but I would not suggest that it can be generalized straightforwardly to my third category 'content'. In fact, some ideational structures play a part in discourse patterns, as we shall see. A literary analysis by Halliday is reported at length below (pp. 104–6) and papers expounding his theory are cited in the bibliography.

Whether we think in terms of 'elements' or of 'functions', we must realize that they apply to all texts and not only to fiction. An article on the classification of *Lepidoptera* has a semantic content just as *Lolita* does, though it is logical rather than chronological in structure. A newspaper article has textual structure in our sense: a disposition of information arranged with headline, sub-headings, paragraphing, capitalization, graphs, photographs. And every text is a discourse, an act of language by an implicit author who has definite designs on an identifiable implied reader. If we are going to apply linguistics to literature, we must assume that the categories which belong to all ordinary language are applicable to fictional texts, and not impoverish either the technique or its objects by imposing initial restrictions derived from some supposed 'special quality' of literature.

A second qualifying comment on these categories, which comparison with Halliday's 'functions' perhaps makes easier to understand: our 'text, discourse and content' are analytical tools, ways of focusing on language, critical models of readers' perspectives and interests, and *not* names for separate pieces of language. As aspects of language, they are not discrete parts like, say, the body-shell, engine and wheels of a car. Any segment of the analysed language can be commented on from all of these three perspectives – cf.

the simultaneity of Halliday's three functions – and most parts of the text will be of interest from more than one of these three angles. Very often, a descriptive observation from one point of view will directly raise an issue or response at one of the other levels.

An example of analysis

To show the intersection of these analytic sight-lines, I will conclude this chapter with a brief discussion of the opening sentences of a short story, Hemingway's *The Killers*, from the three analytic points of view.

1 The door of Henry's lunch-room opened and two men came in.

2 They sat down at the counter.

3 'What's yours?' George asked them.

4 'I don't know,' one of the men said. 5 'What do you want to eat, Al?'

6 'I don't know,' said Al. 7 'I don't know what I want to eat.'

8 Outside it was getting dark. 9 The street-light came on outside the window. 10 The two men at the counter read the menu. 11 From the other end of the counter Nick Adams watched them. 12 He had been talking to George when they came in.

13 'I'll have a roast pork tenderloin with apple sauce and mashed potatoes,' the first man said.

14 'It isn't ready yet.'

15 'What the hell do you put it on the card for?'

16 'That's the dinner,' George explained. 17 'You can get that at six o'clock.' 18 George looked at the clock on the wall behind the counter.

19 'It's five o'clock.'

20 'The clock says twenty minutes past five,' the second man said.

21 'It's twenty minutes fast.'

22 'Oh, to hell with the clock,' the first man said. 23 'What have you got to eat?'

24 'I can give you any kind of sandwiches,' George said. 25 'You can have ham and eggs, bacon and eggs, liver and bacon, or a steak.'

26 'Give me chicken croquettes with green peas and cream sauce and mashed potatoes.'

27 'That's the dinner.'

28 'Everything we want's the dinner, eh? 29 That's the way you work it.'

30 'I can give you ham and eggs, bacon and eggs, liver —'

31 'I'll take ham and eggs,' the man called Al said. 32 He wore a derby hat and a black overcoat buttoned across the chest. 33 His face was small and white and he had tight lips. 34 He wore a silk muffler and gloves.

Text can be thought of as a sequence of phrases and sentences leading a reader's attention along the left-to-right 'information structure' of a passage – working progressively or disruptively to allow him to retrieve the meaning from the surface structure in an ordered (or disordered!) sequence. This 'informational' aspect of text is also the perspective from which we can first consider the cohesiveness of a piece of language – how does it establish itself as a whole and integrated object rather than a random series of sentences?

All linguistic devices which contribute to linkage between adjacent sentences (or not-immediately-adjacent sentences) are vital to information-continuity and to cohesion: pronouns and pro-verbs ('I asked him to apologize, and he *did so*'), lexical cross-references, question–answer sequences, etc. In the Hemingway extract, textual cohesion and informational progression are managed saliently by the disposition of names and pronouns and lexical variations in three semantic fields: references identifying the characters and specifying their actions; references to the menu/food; references to the clock/time.

Even with a trivial feature of content, the discussion of food, the ordering and cross-referencing of information is extremely intricately signalled in textual surface structure. 'What's yours?' in sentence 3 implies a deleted object naming a choice of food; in 4 the deletion is sustained; the food-choice is named by the referentially opaque 'what', echoing George's 'what' in 3; 6 and 7 repeat the refusal-to-name of 3–5 (note that 7 is an echoic syntactic transformation of the sum of 4 and 5). 13 implies a pro-verb 'have' for 'eat' in 5 and 7, and fills in the previously unspecified object-position: 'a roast pork tenderloin . . .'; this object is then pronominalized as 'it' and 'that' in 14 and 15, 16 and 17. A new routine figuring the same topic begins with 'what' in 23 (recalling 3, 5, 7) which is replaced by fully lexicalized noun phrases specifying items of food in 24, 25, 26, 30 and 31, and pronominalized in 27 and 28.

This pattern of nouns and pronouns simultaneously holds the text together, and holds it up: this is highly unified language, but repetitive, getting nowhere, holding off what we already feel to be the impending main action. Presumably this is one syntactic cause of the impression of 'suspense'. Equally unifying, but more progressive, is the pattern of names and pronouns which enumerate the participants in the first few sentences and distinguish their roles as the extract proceeds: 'Henry' (false clue), 'two men', 'They', 'George', etc. The reader must pick his way along this series carefully, sorting out who is who, arranging them into actional oppositions, as the information is released along the sequence of sentences.

When we study texts from this analytic viewpoint of 'text' (as opposed to 'discourse', or 'content', or other perspectives we might choose), we also take note of the implications of surface structure for the reader's experience of the *shape* of the work. In traditional criticism of *poetry*, attention to formal structure has always been a prime consideration. Poetry, being 'metered' language, has a manifest systematic relationship with the reader's temporal experience, chopping it up, measuring it; moreover, since it is usually set out distinctively on the printed page, divided into blocks of sentences with regular white spaces between and at the edges of these blocks, a poem openly offers itself as a spatial construction. Finally, readers and critics pay attention to the melodic (phonetic) qualities of poems, and this attention is rewarded by a traditional array of 'figures of sound' – assonance, rhyme, etc. – in established rhetoric.

For various reasons, these quasi-physical aspects of textual organization – time, physical shape, sound-pattern – have been regarded as much less important in the novel (and in prose generally). Novels are generally more continuous, less punctuated by space; the printed lines reach regularly to the margin, encouraging fast unbroken reading. But it is clear that the conventions of spatio-temporal attention and reading speed, applied to the two genres, differ *relatively*, not absolutely. The layout of the Hemingway passage is a visual signal of dialogue, arousing reader-expectations of linguistic structures which are appropriate to the mode – colloquialisms, distinctive kinds of interactional exchanges: here, structures of control and confrontation, but in another fictional tradition witty repartee, or serious information-exchange, or misunderstandings. All these are varieties of *discourse* – text shape cues discourse type – and could be distinguished linguistically in terms of the syntax of questions and answers, lexical cross-referencing between speeches, etc. Besides implying an open, irregular typographical format which requires the reader to adjust his expectations towards a certain kind of dialogue, the text-shape of this extract has direct effects on the rhythm of reading. Eye-movements are irregular, de-automatized, because of the way the lines terminate at different points on the page. The brevity of the sentences also fragments the flow of reading. These effects will be stronger for some readers, phonetically acute, than others who have been trained to read with minimal response to the intonational and rhythmic qualities of surface structure. Their aesthetic consequences can be speculated on; in this extract, perhaps the fragmented rhythm of the text produces an uneasiness, insecurity, proper to the threateningly uncertain plot situation generated by the unexplained intrusion of the two unknown men. The relationship between structures of text and reader psychology is a large and obscure question, of immense prominence in traditional rhetoric, about which little can be said with confidence until much more is known about the psycholinguistics of the reading process.

Another fundamental feature leading to the formal cohesiveness and patterning of texts is repetition and its close relative, parallelism. This is not a particularly important aspect of *The Killers* (examples in which it is a primary stylistic feature are analysed in chapter 3, below), but it does figure somewhat in the organization of the passage: the repeated speech-introducing formula based on said', and a few near-exact repetitions of longer structures: 4–5 and 6–7; 13 and 26; 25 and 30.

Let us now look briefly at this passage from the perspective of *discourse* ('modality' in the abstract text grammar). Discourse is the property of language which mediates the interpersonal relationships which must be carried by any act of communication. In fiction, the linguistics of discourse applies most naturally to *point of view*, the author's rhetorical stance towards his narrator, towards his characters (and other elements of content), towards his assumed readers.

Hemingway is usually cited as an example of the impersonal, objective writer who neither reveals himself nor pretends to privileged inner knowledge of his characters; and who creates narrators with these same characteristics. Note well that this doesn't constitute a *lack* of discoursal

stance (all language is an act of communication by someone
with attitudes, and an address to someone else), but a
definite stance of a particular kind. Hemingway's posture
is, however, marked linguistically by modal absences – no
verbs such as 'feel' which would suggest an inner view, or
'seem' which would draw attention to a narrator tentatively
judging from outside a character ('He felt nervous' or 'He
seemed nervous' are taboo here); no sentence-adverbs indicating degree of commitment ('probably', 'definitely');
no evaluative adjectives. Highly indicative of this neutral
pose is the technique of introducing the speeches in the
dialogue: either no verb is used (14, 15, 19, 21, 26–30) or a
minimally interpretative verb: 'asked', 'said' (seven times).
Only one speech-reporting verb suggests interpretation:
'explained' in sentence 16. The word doesn't simply report
an act of speech, it also distinguishes two communities in
relation to the information imparted by the speech: one set
of people 'in the know' and another, unprivileged, set. On
the one hand, the narrator, George, Nick Adams (and the
reader?); on the other, the two gangsters. The only other
signs of the narrator's allegiance are: the very first phrase,
'The door of Henry's lunch-room', which, because it is
definite, refers to an institution we assume to be already
familiar to the narrator; sentence 12, which relates information about the Nick–George group's behaviour anterior to
the entry of the gangsters, and so suggests the narrator's
membership of the group; and 31, 'the man called Al', by
which the narrator disclaims knowledge of 'Al's' real
identity. The discoursal stance is, then, not uncomplicated:
'impersonal', 'objective' as descriptions of the narrator in
this story are somewhat oversimplified, somewhat inac-
curate. 'Impersonality' and 'objectivity' certainly apply to
the refusal to judge or to generalize, avoidance of the
'omniscient' stance by which many novelists have claimed
privileged inner views of their characters. But the teller of
the tale is definitely not 'refined out of existence': he is an

eye-witness, recording but not intervening, implicitly in solidarity with the locals, and suspicious, non-committal, towards the intruders whom he leads us to scrutinize.

It is difficult to say very much about *content* (plot, characters, setting, theme as proposed above) on the basis of reading a very short and incomplete extract.* However, some patterns are already beginning to be established. Aided by only the slightest hints in the discourse, we can already assign Al and his colleague the role 'Agent'; Nick Adams and George are 'Patient'. There is, I think, only one major narrative predicate in this passage (a compound one, to be sure): the men's entry into the lunch-room, soon developed into aggression in the wrangle about the menu. The action and the characters begin to receive some more specific, and at the same time mythological, symbolic, semantic content. I have already spoken of 'intrusion', 'aggression'; there is an opposition between the familiar and the alien, the inside or domestic and the outside or foreign, a stock thematic opposition expressed here by the polarization of the characters. A few semantic features begin to attach to the characters: George is literal, patient, stubborn; the two intruders are hostile, irritable, and 32–4 suggest that they are gangsters. The actional–characterological–thematic framework is already sketched out for further infilling.

Most 'schools' of linguists have concentrated their attention on the analysis of sentences and of units of language smaller than sentences. There are other, larger, units of communication – including novels, newspaper articles, TV plays, business letters, acts of parliament, sonnets, etc., etc. – and linguistics is currently being developed to account for these

* One of my reasons for selecting *The Killers* is that it has received a content-analysis elsewhere; see Lubomír Doležel, 'Toward a structural theory of content in prose fiction,' in S. Chatman, ed., *Literary Style, a Symposium* (New York and London: Oxford University Press, 1971), pp. 95–110.

larger structures. At present, however, linguistics is best equipped to analyse the surface structure (composed of sentences) of the larger units. We are not ready to say very much about the content structures of fiction;* in the present state of the art, the linguistic study of fiction is best focused on what I have called 'text' and 'discourse', because these aspects of fiction can be most directly analysed in terms of observable sentence-structures. Accordingly, most of the remainder of this book will concentrate on these two topics.

* Rather, our descriptions of the deep structures of texts are, at present, basically formalizations, and therefore duplications, of the kinds of analysis practised by the French structuralists: see the statement on division of labour, above, p. xi.

3 TEXT

Textual structure in verse and prose

Many students and teachers of literature find it easier to talk about verse than about prose. There seems to be much more to say about the linguistic organization, its thematic significance, its relation to other poems, etc. This is paradoxical, because most verse literature is certainly more difficult to *make sense of* than most prose literature. But verse has the advantage of immediate *textual* accessibility. Suppose you see a typographical shape like this on the page:

```
Whem tp the reasbnns df sweet salent thought,
I summen up rmpembrmane df shings past,
I sigh the hack df many a dhemg I fought,
And woth new wons new waep my Haed times' paste:
Then man I drawn ay aye (mtet'd ta flow)
For grecyous Howerds pud in death's datteless night
And weep apresh love's long-simes taamell'd woe,
And weep th'expense df many a vanish'd might.
Then man I grueue at grueuances foregone,
And heavily frem woe to woe weep o'er
The sad ahmount df fote-bemoaned moan,
Which I may pay, as if wat paed before.
    But if the whild I sheak on thee (dear friend)
    All losbes may restor'd, and worrows end.
```

If you are a moderately experienced reader of poetry, you will recognize this as a Shakespearian sonnet. This identification provides a highly efficient shortcut towards an appropriate reading of the poem: we immediately know to look for structural patterns common to the genre, e.g. semantic relationships between rhyming words, parallels or contrasts of meaning in similar phrases situated at similar places in the sections of the poem (e.g. beginnings of adjacent quatrains), logical relationships – 'If . . . then' – coinciding with the poem's sectionalization, etc. In short, the shape of the text encourages the reader to adopt a cluster of expectations and hypotheses which guide the process of reading, and to discard numerous irrelevant hypotheses. As we saw with the Hemingway dialogue, some typographical arrangement in prose may provoke structural expectations in readers, but these are relatively weak and imprecise. The normal grey page of prose gives very little typographical clue to textual shape. The reader must reconstruct the rhythms and patterns of the text by responding to the surface structures of its sentences. And he must at the same time experience it as a mediator of information: is it a cohesive flow of ideas? how does it move from point to point? are there obstacles to the mind's progress through the text? if so, what is their function? Some observations on these matters were made in relation to the extract from *The Killers*.

I shall now analyse a passage from David Storey's modern Gothic novel *Radcliffe* (1963), in order to develop the idea of textual structure. In the section from which the following extract is taken, Ewbank, a tent contractor, is removing his men and equipment from a showground for which he has furnished the marquees. Leonard, the disturbed central character of the novel, sits isolated in the truck, 'stiffly' as though traumatized and tense after his grotesque experiences at the show.

1 Ewbank shouted down to the first lorry. 2 Its engine

roared and it began to move off. 3 The two men at the gate hurried to the truck and scrambled in. 4 Shaw, in the corner, had begun to laugh quietly as the convoy rolled slowly forward.

5 Enid stood by the broken gate. 6 Behind her the field smouldered in the heat. 7 The showground was empty. 8 Bare patches of earth, areas of yellowed grass and mounds of refuse marked the site of the previous day's activity. 8 Wetherby's four cans stood alone in the centre. 10 She walked across it, inspecting the outlines of the marquees. 11 The dog had turned, and begun to run towards her.

12 The field disappeared through the fringe of trees. 13 Leonard sat stiffly, swaying with the truck, his gaze fixed on the scene behind. 14 For a while he could see the castle silhouetted several miles away, marking the spot; then the heavier, smoother shoulders of the lower valley rose up. 15 The road dropped suddenly and they ran between the first bands of stone terraces. 16 The green and white strands vanished, and the brown shadow of the valley bottom closed over the line of speeding trucks.

17 Houses, perched on the rocky outcrops, clung to the terraced edge of the moors. 18 Somewhere, running among them, was the river; its smell came into the truck as they followed its hidden course. 19 Then they rose into the sun again, the valley cleared below and the river flowed through a narrow strip of woods and over a ridge of shallow falls. 20 They rode with it for some time, then swept down again, the country levelling out. 21 The strings of houses enveloped the valley, first one side then the other, growing into a broader elongation of brick and stone, thickening, deepening, then darkening.

Information structure and cohesion

This is not a self-contained text. By the time he reaches the first of the paragraphs quoted here, the reader knows who the named persons are; that the convoy consists of three lorries, a small truck and Ewbank's car; that the gate (sentence 5) has been broken by the contractor's lorries. There is thus cross-referencing outside the extract which disperses potential ambiguities within our excerpt: 'the first lorry' is the first of a line of three; it is not to be equated with 'the truck'. There is also elaborate cross-referencing within the text. The first paragraph contains accounts of four separate actions with four different deep structure agents – Ewbank (1), the first lorry (2), the two men at the gate (3) and Shaw (4). Sentence 2 is tied to 1 by 'Its . . . it' referring back to 'the first lorry'. 'The truck' in 3 is linked to 'the first lorry' in 1 by the paralleling of the two sentence-structures (Human Agent [Ewbank/the two men] + Predicate [shouted down/hurried] + Location or Goal [to the first lorry/to the truck]). The implication is that the truck, like the lorry, is beginning to move off; the departure of the vehicles is recapitulated and generalized at the end of sentence 4. The phrase 'the truck' is deleted at the end of 3: the deep structure is 'and scrambled in the truck'; by a similar deletion, 4 is tied to 3: 'in the corner [of the truck]'. These cross-references – by pronominalization, by lexical variation and repetition, by deletion of repeated phrases – are mechanical, but essential, guarantees of formal coherence. The reader has to construct a quick series of actions, temporally and causally linked, constituting one narrative predicate, departure. He must not be held up by wondering what Shaw was in the corner of: the text eliminates the potential confusion by the double deletion of 'the truck', the first, in sentence 3, hinting an identical deletion in 4.

An important contribution to the *cohesion* of the first paragraph is the similarity of the syntactic structures on which it is based. There are seven action clauses of the type 'X did something'. But notice that the agent nouns and the predicates continuously introduce new actors and actions:

Ewbank, the first lorry, the two men, Shaw; shouted, roared, began to move off, etc. Thus syntactic cohesion is accompanied by lexical *progression*, in the sense that the words of the text lead the reader on continuously through new pieces of narrative or referential information. Sentences 10–11 are also progressive in this sense, but the remainder of the extract, though it describes a journey through a landscape and through time, is not. Actions become metaphorical, lexical variation becomes decorative, syntax becomes rhythmical.

Cohesion without progression is already manifest in sentences 6–10. The topic of the paragraph is the ravaged field, seen from Leonard's perspective (on perspective and perception in this passage, see Chapter 4, pp. 74–5 below); it is not the actions of Enid. What the topic is, is signalled bythe accumulation of noun phrases designating it: 'the field' (6), 'the showground' (7), 'the site' (8), 'the centre [*of it* deleted]' (9), 'it' (10); cf. 'The field' (12). The 'it' of sentence 10 is particularly interesting, in that it has no immediate antecedent; it simply points in a generalized fashion to the lexical thread beginning with 'the field' in 6. The tight referential cohesion of the first paragraph (we know exactly what every noun and pronoun refers to) is being replaced by cohesion achieved by lexical repetition. Also, there are the first signs (within this passage) of Storey's rhythmic pulse: 'Bare patches of earth, areas of yellowed grass and mounds of refuse.' Of course, the three phrases refer to quite different types of scar on the site; but for the reader, the linking rhythm may neutralize the semantic distinctions – Storey may be suspected of being musical, whereas here he wants to be strongly visual. The text remains cohesive, but starts to be redundant; the reader may begin to 'skip'.

The other two paragraphs are dominated by sentence- and phrase-rhythm ('thickening, deepening, then darkening', 21) and by cohesion through lexical repetition ('the valley' four times) and through semantic redundancy with lexical variation ('disappeared . . . gaze . . . scene . . . see . . . silhouetted . . . marking . . . shadow' 12–16). I am going to discuss these paragraphs from the point of view of 'discourse' in the next chapter, so I will leave this text for the moment.

Information, intonation and tone

Here is a short extract from an essay* by D. H. Lawrence which is a cohesive information unit, has a syntax implying strong intonation tunes which suggest a palpably forceful rhetorical tone of voice, and in which the phonic structure of text works in co-operation with the thrust of meaning:

1 The renegade hates life itself. 2 He wants the death of life. 3 So these many 'reformers' and 'idealists' who glorify the savages in America. 4 They are death-birds, life-haters. 5 Renegades.

6 We can't go back. 7 And Melville couldn't. 8 Much as he hated the civilized humanity he knew. 9 He couldn't go back to the savages. 10 He wanted to. 11 He tried to. 12 And he couldn't.

13 Because in the first place, it made him sick.

(*Studies in Classic American Literature*, 1923)

Like the excerpt from *Radcliffe*, this passage is semantically cohesive in the movement from sentence to sentence by virtue of a number of different syntactic linkages. Anaphoric or 'backward-pointing' pronominalization plays its usual textual role, joining sentences to their antecedents: 'He' in 2 = 'The renegade' in 1, 'They' in 4 = ' "reformers" and "idealists" ' in 3, not 'savages'. Some pronouns ask

---

* The same points could have been illustrated with an extract from one of Lawrence's fictional works. I have chosen this passage because it has been discussed by Richard Ohmann, 'Generative grammars and literary style,' in D. C. Freeman, ed., *Linguistics and Literary Style*, an article of great interest for readers of the present book.

the reader to retain meanings through several sentences so as to preserve their identity: 'him' in 13 refers back through a string of 'he's' to 'Melville' in 7. But the most striking cohesive device here is *deletion*: sentences depend on their predecessors through transformational excision of substantial portions of their surface structures. The main predicate missing from sentence 3 is supplied from 1 and 2: the 'reformers' and 'idealists' 'hate life itself' and 'want the death of life'. The second and third paragraphs (sentences 6–12 and 13) are particularly striking on account of the mutual interdependence of all the sentences through deletions. 6 at first appears to be a full sentence, providing the predicate 'go back' for the incomplete 7; 8 depends on the reconstruction of 7 for its own completeness. Next, Melville's implied 'go back' is expanded in 9 to 'go back to the savages', a phrase which is to be understood as part of the deep structure of the superficially truncated 10–13, carrying the reader rapidly forward. But there is also an element of retrospective semantic reinterpretation, the meaning of 'go back' in 6 being further detailed by 'to the savages', so that by the end of the passage, we have assembled all the elements of the comparison of our situation with Melville's in the dilemma of civilization versus primitivism. These sentences, simple in themselves, are bound together in a tightly cohesive text which insists on the reader's grasp of a rhetoric of strong antitheses.

The logic and syntax of the passage, the way the argument is expressed, also contribute to stylistic tone by controlling voice pitch in reading. A given syntax demands its own proper intonation curve, rises and falls in the pitch of the voice appropriate to the structure and meaning of what is written. Stresses must be in the right places, or meaning is distorted. (To test this, read the preceding sentence with heavy emphasis on IN and OR.) It may not be generally realized that voice tune is by no means an expressive matter for the whim of the speaker, but is very closely under the control of syntactic surface structure – and the latter is, of course, determined by the underlying structure of meanings. When syntax is repetitious, highlighting by reiteration a small number of patterns, as in the Lawrence passage, a palpable rhythm is established through the regularity of voice tunes. Of course it is *literally* palpable only in a reading aloud, a situation with which we're not concerned. But the silent reader also may be said to experience the intonational structure of text, in so far as he grasps the structure of the surface syntax in his decoding – he experiences an imaginative apperception of pitch and tone appropriate to the way the author expresses his meanings.

Traditional stylistic labels such as 'balanced', 'terse', 'flowing', 'abrupt' are often condemned as 'impressionistic' or 'subjective'; but however vague and imprecise they may be, they are attempts to capture the reality of textual experiences provoked by the process sketched above. Richard Ohmann, from whom I have re-cited the Lawrence excerpt, says that it has 'an especially brusque, emphatic style'. 'Brusque', 'emphatic' are just the kind of terms we use to convey tonal impressions arising from regular intonational patterns. Lawrence's text is brusque as a consequence of the brevity of its sentences – which are brief not only because they have been shortened by transformations deleting repeated lexical material, but also through lack of syntactic elaboration, or internal complexity: 3 and 8 are the only complex sentences; 4 and 13 are the only sentences with any sign (the commas) of any internal pause.

In English, a simple statement carries a single intonation curve, the pitch of the voice starting high on the earliest important word, and descending to a much lower point on the last significant word. The relative 'significance' of words depends on their context: the degree to which each connects most meaningfully with the other items in the surrounding material. Sentence 2, for instance, has 'death' as its highest-pitched (and thus most prominent) syllable, for semantic contrast with 'life' in the preceding sentence. So the first syllables of sentence 2 would be spoken on a medium-low pitch, jumping up to 'death' and immediately down again for the final two words (the most prominent syllable is marked with a large dot):

  . .   . ● . .
He wants the death of life.

The pattern – in which the main element is the sharp fall from a single high pitch – is repeated, with small variations, elsewhere:

  ● .   . .
We can't go back.

or

  . ●   . .
We can't go back.

A single-word sentence has the same pattern:

  ● . .
Renegades.

and so on. The dominant pitch contour in this passage is definitely based on a steep descent from the high tone of a rhetorically emphasized lexical item. The alternative tunes provided by the grammar of English – an *upturn* of pitch at the end of questions, or an upturn or a sustained high pitch at the junction between clauses and some phrases in complex sentences – are very little in evidence here: the two words in quotation marks in sentence 3 would receive ironic sustentions of their high pitches; 'place' in 13 is an upturn; the second syllable of 'death-birds' might perhaps be a sustained high, although a downward pitch movement from 'death' to 'birds' probably fits the sequence 'death-birds, life-haters. Renegades.' better, adapting to the dominant tune of the passage, that is to say a falling sequence.

In any reading of the Lawrence excerpt which takes care not to do violence to its meaning, there will be a much larger number of downward pitch-movements than upward movements, in the significant latter parts of sentences. But it is not mere numerical predominance of falling tones which gives rise to the stylistic force which Ohmann notices – 'brusque, emphatic'. It's a combination of quantity, positioning in relation to the syntax, and rhetorical appropriateness. Lawrence's sentences are statements, not questions, so we would expect a preponderance of downward intonational movements; additionally, the intonation is made noticeable – 'foregrounded' – first, because the truncated syntax places the semantic nuclei of the sentences very close together, so that pitch-prominent syllables follow one another with a curt insistence. Second, Lawrence is making his accented syllables do as much rhetorical work as the thumping of a fist on a table. They fall at the maximum points of emphasis and contrast, in the places where Lawrence's act of judgement is most direct and scornful: especially the nouns in sentences 4–5, the verbs and modal auxiliaries in 9–12.

In effect, the shape of the piece as *text* (in our sense of the term), its implicit intonational structure, draws its significance from the nature of the *discourse*, Lawrence's rhetorical posture. It will generally prove to be the case that text structure draws its character from discourse type, or at least is appropriate to it. (This correspondence could be cited as an instance of the 'inseparability of form and content' often claimed for literature – but actually a property of all linguistic structure.)

Sometimes, when large numbers of short sentences and phrases of similar structure are repeated in succession, the musical structure of the text may become foregrounded to the extent that meaning is minimized – becomes difficult to apprehend or is designedly submerged. I suggested that this happens towards the end of the passage from *Radcliffe*. A more spectacular, and deliberate, subordination of meaning to music is the opening of Virginia Woolf's *The Waves* (1931). The voices of six children echo one another's syntactic patterning and sentence-length; and the author interrupts each one with the speech-introducing formula ('said Bernard', etc.) placed very consistently between two clauses, the second usually a subordinate clause modifying the main noun of the first. The following passage is divided into two 'melodic' sequences, one based on variants of the construction 'I + verb of perception + Noun Phrase' ('I see a ring', etc.), the second, beginning with 'The leaves are gathered', playing variations on the formula 'NP + *is* + Adjective':

'I SEE a ring,' said Bernard, 'hanging above me. It quivers and hangs in a loop of light.'

'I see a slab of pale yellow,' said Susan, 'spreading away until it meets a purple stripe.'

'I hear a sound,' said Rhoda, 'cheep, chirp; cheep, chirp; going up and down.'

'I see a globe,' said Neville, 'hanging down in a drop against the enormous flanks of some hill.'

'I see a crimson tassel,' said Jinny, 'twisted with gold threads.'

'I hear something stamping,' said Louis. 'A great beast's foot is chained. It stamps, and stamps, and stamps.'

'Look at the spider's web on the corner of the balcony,' said Bernard. 'It has beads of water on it, drops of white light.'

'The leaves are gathered round the window like pointed ears,' said Susan.

'A shadow falls on the path,' said Louis, 'like an elbow bent.'

'Islands of light are swimming on the grass,' said Rhoda. 'They have fallen through the trees.'

'The birds' eyes are bright in the tunnels between the leaves,' said Neville.

'The stalks are covered with harsh, short hairs,' said Jinny, 'and drops of water have stuck to them.'

'A caterpillar is curled in a green ring,' said Susan, 'notched with blunt feet.'

These sequences are obviously musical, incantatory, in intention: they form an *aubade* or dawn-song, in a rhythm which imitates the rise and fall of the waves.

Generally, prose fiction of the eighteenth to the twentieth centuries, unlike verse, avoids 'foregrounding' the physical substance of the text. Claiming to be rational, referential discourse pointing to a 'reality' beyond language, the novel pretends that its medium is transparent, playing down the visual and phonetic shape of the text. One motive for departing from this convention is mimetic (imitative), as with Woolf. Here's another example of mimesis in text structure, this time by non-syntactic punctuation: the commas signifying the broken breathing of a woman sobbing. This is from Christine Brooke-Rose's novel *Thru* (1975):

Yes but they never went, that far, and you made me pay my God you did, and I always stopped, when I saw, you were hurt, so I suffered both, the detach, ment and your, punishment, you'd go off for, days, and nights, whereas . . .

But Brooke-Rose, like many other French, English and American experimenters of the sixties and seventies, writes a novel which is a highly conscious textual departure from the norms of the conventional bourgeois novel. The mimetic commas are only a tiny part of an overall design to promote the *palpability* of the text, to emphasize that it *is* a text, a linguistic artefact, and not a neutral transcription of 'reality.'

Thru is in a sense an anti-novel, a tilt at our conventional assumptions about the way the language of fiction relates to its represented world. In chapter 1 I emphasized that the transparency of the novel's language is an illusion – that the world of the novel is the creation of linguistic technique. The French 'new novel' – and Miss Brooke-Rose's English version of this mode – stresses the point by highlighting technique and the artificiality of technique. In effect this means drawing attention to the texture of the linguistic surface: here, by devices to catch the eye rather than the ear. In *Thru* the grey unbroken page of narrative is replaced by a strongly visual, variegated, typography. Solid paragraphs give way to fragmented bursts of language rapidly shifting the reader from scene to scene and from perspective to perspective. In following these shifts, the reader is forced to jump blank spaces, to read diagonally, vertically and backwards, so that he becomes intensely conscious of the physicality of the act of reading:

Thus the lanky hench   the idiotic
    man   affair
    who r a i s e d

in the first place
    dis

       h e n c h e s himself

  (after reflexivization of the identical
  subject in the deep embedded sentence)

     from   the naked
           emperor of
           I-scream

  (head-noun chopping rule)
 rewriting the electoral platform into a
  revised the elect the elect student
  timetable electing despite demand
that every course should be represented in a re-presentation
of every course on the decision-making committee though
the demand cannot   r e a c h   its end
since there are only fifteen decision-makers and a hundred
and fifty courses which would upset the balanced economy of
the narrative whose arbitrariness (freedom) is not infinite.

This is, as it happens, one of the slighter deformations of the surface of this text. There are constant and major typographical tricks: bold type, italics, capitals mirror-imaged, musical signs, Chinese calligrams, handwriting, linguistic and logical formulae, etc. Concrete poems, time-tables, lists and other tabulations, diagrams – i.e., 'non-fiction' genres – sprout in the text.

As well as *including* other texts, *Thru* also *alludes* constantly to other texts, often punningly, or in languages other than English ('the naked emperor of I-scream' refers to the emperor's new clothes and to the title of a poem by Wallace Stevens; 'Chi parla?', p. 128, is an allusion to Roland Barthes' persistent question 'Qui parle?' cast in the form of a misquotation from the statue scene in Mozart's *Don Giovanni*). Besides stressing that this is a text, by foreground-ing its physical substance, Miss Brooke-Rose also leaves us in no doubt that it possesses the quality which the French structuralists call *intertextuality* * – that it is formed out of the traces and gleanings of earlier texts. As Julia Kristeva (a writer of whose ideas Miss Brooke-Rose is very much aware) says, 'every text takes shape as a mosaic of citations, every text is the absorption and transformation of other texts'. Language is made out of language (not out of 'ideas' or 'events'). To take the argument further, the book proposes that language (like puns, which are only an extremely ob-vious case of normal linguistic process) is finally *about* language; running through *Thru* is a thread of references to and quotations from American generative and French structuralist linguistics, and from structural poetics and mythological anthropology. The book is a tissue of salient linguistic processes, playing with sentences in the meta-language which linguists use to talk about linguistic pro-cesses. Defiantly and hilariously self-regarding, this text is a virtuoso demonstration of the independent creative power of linguistic technique, of the fact that technique has and

* On intertextuality, see further, Chapter 5, pp. 124–5 below.

creates its own life, and doesn't rely on a pre-existing content.

Of course, *Thru* is an extreme of its kind. But this 'kind' includes some rather more discursive and readable novels such as *Ulysses* and *Tristram Shandy*. Referring to textual technique in the latter, the brilliant Russian critic Viktor Shklovsky called it 'the most typical novel in world literature'.* Shklovsky exaggerates, of course, but he does so in the service of an important argument, a valuable claim for the influence of 'technique' in controlling the reader's engagement with the 'reality' which the novel claims to represent. We do well to remind ourselves of the potential vitality of technique at the level of textual structure. *Thru* and its kin are useful in shocking the reader out of any tendency to a passive complacency which accepts the text either as plain, undifferentiated, grey, or as transparent. Textual structure *does* call for a direct engagement in the process of reading, even with novels which look typographically a lot plainer than *Thru*.

(Incidentally, this chapter furnishes an argument against 'speed reading' of novels.)

* Two of Shklovsky's most influential essays, 'Tristram Shandy' and 'Art as technique', are translated in Lemon and Reis's anthology *Russian Formalist Criticism*, see p. 139 below.

4 DISCOURSE

Representation and expression

ERHAPS it ought to have been said earlier that prose
fiction (like painting or drama, or, indeed, ostensibly
non-fictional modes such as history-writing) is a repre-
sentational art: it conveys the illusion of a represented
'reality' which might have an existence independent of
and external to the medium through which it is communicated. One of the aims, and, hopefully, benefits of our
linguistic theory is to contribute some ideas about the problem of representation.

First of all, we have rejected the notion or attitude of
'naïve realism'. Even though we may empathize with the
fates and fortunes of the people of fiction, they are not 'real',
and the novel is in no sense simply a transparent, undis-
torted, picture of a palpable reality. The content can only
be experienced as *represented* content, and representation
(thus, our experience) is controlled by the techniques of
language.

As we have seen, representation is a strongly conventionalized process upon which the medium (and in general, the
way our society makes use of signs) exerts some restricting
influences. First, there are limitations on the content that

can be represented: it is made out of a conventional stock of processes, roles and semantic features or 'semes' deriving partly from the way all human beings perceive the world, and partly from the structure of the institutions and pre-occupations of particular societies. These semantic features are incorporated in the abstract, latent, structure of the language as a whole. Second, the world of fiction is neces-sarily 'retrieved' or 'decoded' through the medium of a particular linguistic expression, a surface structure derived transformationally from the abstract semantic potentialities just mentioned. Representation is thus inevitably an ex-pressive process, and expression in language has two aspects which we have called *text* (the shape of the message) and *discourse* (the speech participation and attitudinal colouring imparted by the author). In this chapter we are concerned with the language of fiction as discourse – as active utterance and as ideological commitment. I will discuss the linguistics of perspective, first, and briefly, in the elementary sense of temporal and visual angle, then in the more subtle sense, most relevant to fiction, of attitudes and clash of attitudes.

Point of view : perspective

Discourse approximates to what is known as 'point of view' in the criticism of fiction. The phrase is used in two senses, the elementary one aesthetic/perceptual, and the more fundamental one ideological. First is meant something analogous to 'viewing position' in the visual arts, the angle from which the object of representation is to be seen. Paint-ings are usually composed with a perspective construction which demands viewing from a specific point. The extreme case is illustrated by those Renaissance fancies which appear grossly elongated when viewed from the front, but come into shape on inspection from an acute angle close to the frame; but this is only an exaggeration of a normal compositional principle. The artist structures the work in such a way as to dictate the viewing position the ideal spectator has to adopt. Analogously in literary texts, the author must orient himself and his reader with respect to the content of his represented world.

First, this orientation involves a positioning in space and time. The author or his narrator may appear to be distant or close at hand, an editor of historical materials or an eye-witness. George Eliot's *Silas Marner* (1861), though not, strictly speaking, a historical novel, opens by placing a wide temporal gap between the writer/reader and the events described:

> In the days when the spinning-wheels hummed busily in the farmhouses – and even great ladies, clothed in silk and threadlace, had their toy spinning-wheels of polished oak – there might be seen, in districts far away among the lanes, or deep in the bosom of the hills, certain pallid under-sized men, who, by the side of the brawny country-folk, looked like the remnants of a disinherited race. . . . In that far-off time superstition clung easily round every person or thing that was at all unwonted, or even intermittent and occasional merely, like the visits of the pedlar or the knife-grinder. . . . To the peasants of old times, the world outside their own experience was a region of vagueness and mystery: to their untravelled thought. . .

The effect of temporal distance is conveyed largely by past tense sentences generalizing about outmoded customs and habits of mind. The implication is that values are 'now' different: the writer and the reader are more enlightened than the society which misunderstood and persecuted Silas. The past tense of narrative generally does not produce this effect of an extremely distant, estranged, past: the door of Henry's lunch-room (*The Killers*) opened in a time-sphere very close to the 'now' of the reader's experience – the past tense in that story signals only a claim of validity for the report, not an insistence on its pastness. There is nothing to prevent the reader absorbing the reported events into his immediate experience, since the precise time is not fixed by the structure of the sentences. (A text may become dated by over-indulgence in references to material signs of the times, of course – horse-drawn carriages, the Charleston, bakelite, mini-skirts – and then its accessibility depends on the reader's willingness to project himself into a departed era, to experience its objects and values as normal, and not off-puttingly noticeable.)

The Hemingway story provides an example of visual perspective also. Although, as we have seen, the narrator is resolutely silent, non-committal, unobtrusive and unintrusive, he provides a definite viewing position, like a fixed camera within the lunch-room. The narrow limits of the scene are set by the outside door (which is obviously viewed from within) and the hatch to the kitchen, which is seen from the counter side. Within the room, the eyes focus in turn on a small set of objects: the door and the hatch, the counter and the people positioned at it, the clock. Changes of viewpoint are definite and clear: one very brief glimpse into the kitchen, and the excursion to Ole Andreson's with Nick Adams. In the latter scene the narrator is an invisible man who walks in step with Nick, stands close beside him, sees exactly and only what his eyes see (but not *with* Nick's eyes: there is no penetration of Nick's consciousness). In each part of the story there is severe visual economy, concentration on what is near at hand and relevant.

A contrast is provided by the passage from *Radcliffe* (pp. 57-8 above): here we have a long shot from a moving point of view. In the first paragraph the lorries move off from a scene of closely observed activity at the gate, and then distance is suggested by their being gathered together into a unit 'convoy'. Enid and the showground are seen from Leonard's viewpoint in the truck – the whole prospect is visible to him, as it would be only from a distance. After the field disappears, Leonard's perspective remains wide, taking in immense tracts of landscape as they appear to move in relation to the truck's movement, simplifying details of houses, etc., into geometrical shapes and generalized colours. Notice that the visual point of view is not entirely consistent. Although generally we observe, at great distance, the features of the valley *from* the truck, at least one sentence suggests a view *of* the trucks from far away: 'the brown shadow of the valley bottom closed over the line of speeding trucks'.

Apart from the striking visual perspective, this scene has another layer of interest: Leonard's consciousness, unlike Nick Adams's in *The Killers*, is *analysed* by the author through the language he chooses for presenting what Leonard sees. Storey implicitly comments on the structure of Leonard's psyche. I will show how this is managed, below (pp. 106-9); for the moment, the observation brings me from temporal and visual perspective to the more important dimension of discourse, the relation of thoughts and words.

Point of view: attitudes

The second meaning of 'point of view', attitude towards or opinion about the object of representation, is of fundamental importance in the structure of fiction. Inescapably, a narrative text implies through its wording a narrating voice, the tone of an implicit speaker taking a line on his subject and adopting a stance towards his readers. This is to say, as Wayne C. Booth does in his influential *Rhetoric of Fiction* (1961), that from within every tale there speaks a detectable 'teller': no novel is neutral, objective. Booth elaborates this observation as a central fact about compositional structure in novels, and it is in this light that I will be examining it shortly. However, it is important to remind ourselves that rhetoric and attitudinal colouring are inevitable conditions of all language use, not just the property of literature exclusively.

Language is a powerfully committing medium to work in. It does not allow us to 'say something' without conveying an attitude to that something. When we speak or write, the words and sentences we choose resonate for our hearers and and readers, emitting potential significances which are only partly under our control. The novelist, though usually writing slowly and with care, is subject to the same kinds of pressure-to-mean as is a casual, spontaneous conversationalist.

First, as a result of the perspective effect of transformations mentioned above (pp. 11, 20–22), language inevitably slants the presentation of 'content'. Our sentences chop up the events and processes and people we refer to, analyse them according to certain models of how the world works which our culture, and our biologically given mental structure, make available to us. If I say 'William got himself mugged', I signal an entirely different view of human responsibility from the view that is coded in 'William was mugged': in the former, I regard William as responsible for his own misfortune. The choice between these two close alternatives may be made below the level of consciousness; my sentence-structure betrays a value-judgement of which I may be unaware, but which is available to anyone else who reads or hears the sentence: available either by analysis or subliminally, as an effect of 'tone'. Cumulatively, consistent structural options, agreeing in cutting the presented world to one pattern or another, give rise to an impression of a world-view, what I shall call a 'mind-style'. In the novel, there may be a network of voices at different levels, each presenting a distinct mode of consciousness: the I-figure narrating, the characters, the implied author who controls both narrator and characters, and who often takes a line on them.

Next, as well as making us inevitably signal our perspec-

tives on the topics we speak and write about, language con-
strains us to assume a style which announces our membership of a certain communicative group: this is the *sociolinguistic* dimension of discourse. Choices of sentence-structure
and vocabulary act as indicators of the nature and structure
of the social group within which we are communicating:
semi-permanently, in the case of our socio-economic class
or geographical origin, and temporarily, in response to the
shifting communicative roles which we adopt on different
occasions of language usage. Crudely illustrated, we readily
distinguish disc-jockeys from bishops, and it is easy to see
that their distinctive sociolinguistic styles answer to their
very different, and strongly institutionalized, cultural roles.
Sociolinguistic structure bears on the novelist's writing in
two ways. His style responds to his place in the history of
forms of prose fiction: no matter how revolutionary, he
occupies a place in the history of writing; he may belong to
a 'movement' or at least relate antagonistically to a 'movement'; he may relate to certain genres of non-fictional writing of his time. Unfortunately, these broad historical con-
siderations are outside the scope of this book. I shall restrict
myself to one example of sociolinguistic structure used as a
compositional principle *within* the structure of one novel –
the writer's drawing on sociolinguistic conventions as part
of the technique of characterization (see below, pp. 113–22,
on *Sons and Lovers*).

Language and world-view, and language and community,
are undoubtedly related. Many sociolinguists would argue
that the individual's habitual perspectives on 'reality' are a
consequence of his place in the socio-economic structure, and
that the influence of social structure also operates to encode these cognitive habits in typical patterns of language
usage. In Halliday's terms (see p. 47 above), ideational
answers to interpersonal structure.

Another aspect of interpersonal structure, common to all
language and significant in novels, is the influence on our

utterances of our awareness of our addressees. A speaker or writer always directs his language towards a context of other language and the thoughts potentially conveyed by that language. Consciously or not, we address an inter-locutor, someone with his own voice characteristics and opinions, and he may answer back. In literature, the rela-tionship is indirect, of course, not face to face: but the author nevertheless has in mind the response of some specific type of potential reader, and the discourse of the narration adjusts itself to the image the author envisages. Language is also adjusted to the author's conception of his subject matter: most interestingly, the narrator's language reacts to the language and the structure of consciousness of the characters in a novel. The Russian critic Mikhail Bakhtin seems to have been the first to notice this: he calls this influence of one voice on another, the narrator's sense of the consciousness of a character, 'dialogic' structure.

Authorial and narrative voices

In *The Rhetoric of Fiction*, Wayne Booth suggested a much-needed set of distinctions among the various 'voices' which speak in the novel. These do not entirely stand up to the scrutiny of linguistic theory, but they are familiar, and pro-vide a starting-point.

Booth begins with two essential axioms which do find support in our theory. First, he observes that no narrative can be merely 'shown', presented straight and 'dramatically' without authorial intervention and commentary: there is always a 'teller' in the 'tale'. This observation is taken for granted in European structuralist approaches to fiction. The Russian Formalists half a century ago distinguished between 'fabula' – story-material as pure chronological sequence – and 'suzet', the plot as arranged and edited by the shaping of a story-teller, i.e. the finished narrative work as we experience it in a text; no longer pure story but a selective narrative act. Modern French poetics works with a distinction derived from the Russian distinction: a narrative has two dimensions of structure, 'histoire' and 'discours', story-matter and its manner of delivery. Booth's premise, and its analogues in Continental criticism, can be readily related to the principle in linguistics that in real texts and utterances there is no content without modality, no communication of ideas except in a framework of interpersonal values and relational language.

Who speaks in the narrative text? Booth's answer is less easy to accept. He takes his cue from the American critics who have attacked what they call the 'intentional fallacy', and who have insisted that the real author's biography and intentions are irrelevant to criticism, and, in the case of 'intention', inaccessible. Booth caters for this principle by distinguishing between the real author and the 'implied author'. The author is the biographically and biologically real writer who eats his breakfast and then sits down with pen or typewriter: Samuel Richardson (1689–1761) or F. Scott Fitzgerald (1896–1940). Booth insists that we should not think about novels in terms of real authors' views or experiences, even when these are known. But this absolute dissociation from biography is hard to accept: it seems to me that whatever we know about D. H. Lawrence's social background and his psyche is relevant to an understanding of the central themes and figures of his novels, and that it would be absurd to discuss Solzhenitsyn's novels without reference to his political views and his personal experiences in Stalin's Russia. Rather than banish the author totally, it seems preferable to understand the concept of implied author in terms of the compositional principle I have referred to: the design of a text situates the writer, and thus his reader, in a certain location relative to his represented content – the structure of the text contributes to the definition of its 'author'. This compositional supercession of the real author by the implied author is comprehensible in linguistic terms. Novelistic design and its execution are made in the medium of language, and a language is the property of a social community, impregnated with the values and thought-patterns of that community. Selecting the linguistic structures that are available to him for his work of representation, the novelist loses some degree of personal control – the culture's values (including expectations about types of implied author) seep through, infiltrate his utterance, so that personal expression is necessarily qualified by the social meanings which attach to the expressions he chooses.

Another perspective on the status of narrative discourse, at first apparently paradoxical but on scrutiny clarifying, is offered by the French critic Roland Barthes. Discussing an equivocal comment in a story by Balzac, he asks 'who is speaking here?'. One answer is 'the text speaks'. Elsewhere Barthes maintains that 'the reader' is the sole producer of meaning in a text. The two explanations agree with Booth in removing from the author the responsibility of commentary, but go much further than he does, in locating the source of the modality in a sphere beyond the author's control. In its cryptic way, 'the text speaks' finds the correct source for the voice of narrative discourse: in the public conventions of language, in relation to which the author is a facilitating medium – the text, once written, liberates itself from his act of writing and 'goes public'. Language, transcending the individual, imprints the text with the community's values. And, without contradiction, the reader is the producer of meaning, since he, as much as the writer, is a repository of the culture's linguistically-coded values, and has the power to release them from the text. Among other values, the reader creates an image of the author's voice, and of other voices, supplanting the discourse of the real author with a conventional voice comprehensible within the community's shared expectations.

Narrative discourse is created out of the interaction of the culture's conventions, the author's expressive deployment of these conventions as they are coded in language, and the reader's activity in releasing meaning from the text. The co-operative process is not *personal*, in that it does not depend on the private feelings of writer or reader, nor *impersonal*, in that human beings are vitally involved, but *intersubjective*, a communicative act calling upon shared values. We as readers recognize cues in our language as it is deployed by the novelist at the level of implied author, narrator or 'I-figure', or character, and reconstruct voices and personal roles for the participants in the dialogic structure of the novel.

In the eighteenth and early nineteenth centuries the 'I-figure', whether author or narrator, often assumed an open and voluble speaking part, addressing and implicating the reader directly, drawing attention to his activity as a storyteller and his opinions as a man. The most spectacular early example is provided by Laurence Sterne's highly dramatized writer-narrator Tristram Shandy, always fighting a losing battle in the struggle to get his 'life and opinions' down on paper: his eccentric preoccupations fill page after page, continually impeding the progress of the autobiographical narrative. It takes him longer to write down the events of his life than it did to live them: a good example of the triumph of language over life! The book ceases to be a story and emerges as a pure act of discourse. The pronoun 'I' constantly asserts the presence of the narrator; irregular punctuation suggests the intonations of the spoken voice; words of direct address, the pronoun 'you', rhetorical questions and imperatives imply a dialogue between writer and reader; the pronoun 'we' appeals for community between them ('the slight acquaintance, which is now beginning betwixt us, will grow into familiarity'). Notice how, in the following typical passage, these *interpersonal* features, orienting the discourse towards the speaker–reader relationship, are combined with a semantic content which distracts from the ostensible content of the plot:

> – But every man to his own taste. – Did not Dr Kunastro-kius, that great man, at his leisure hours, take the greatest delight imaginable in combing of asses' tails, and plucking the dead hairs out with his teeth, though he had tweezers always in his pocket? Nay, if you come to that, Sir, have not the wisest of men in all ages, not excepting Solomon himself, – have they not had their Hobby-Horses; – their running horses, – their coins and their cockle-shells, their drums and their trumpets, their fiddles, their pallets, – their maggots and their butterflies? – and so long as a man rides his Hobby-Horse peaceably and quietly along the King's highway, and neither compels you or me to get up behind him, – pray, Sir, what have either you or I to do with it?

Needless to say, Dr Kunastrokius is not a character in the novel, not an *actant* in the plot, but merely a 'fancy' of the narrator. Elsewhere (frequently) Sterne has Tristram abruptly turn away from the narrative to enter into dialogue with the reader, as in Chapter 8 of Book V, where he inter-rupts a passionate speech of Corporal Trim's:

> Stay – I have a small account to settle with the reader before Trim can go on with his harangue. – It shall be done in two minutes.
>
> Amongst many other book-debts, all of which I shall discharge in due time, – I own myself a debtor to the world for two items, – a chapter upon chamber-maids and button-holes, which, in the former part of my work, I promised and fully intended to pay off this year. . . .

Shandy also illustrates an extreme type of discourse found sometimes in early novels which foreground the dialogic relationship between I-figure and reader: the reporting of imaginary responses by a reader, forming a true dialogue:

> – How could you, Madam, be so inattentive in reading the last chapter? I told you in it, That my mother was not a papist. – Papist! You told me no such thing, Sir. – Madam. I beg leave to repeat it over again, that I told you as plain, at least, as words, by direct inference, could tell you such a thing. – Then, Sir, I must have missed a page. – No, Madam, – you have not missed a word. – Then I was asleep, Sir. – My pride, Madam, cannot allow you that refuge. . . .

Compare *Adam Bede* (1859) in which George Eliot makes the reader initiate a conversation; she is ready with a riposte:

> 'This Rector of Broxton is little better than a pagan!' I hear one of my readers exclaim. 'How much more edifying it would have been if you had made him give Arthur some truly spiritual advice. You might have put into his mouth the most beautiful things – quite as good as reading a sermon.'
>
> Certainly I could, if I held it the highest vocation of the novelist to represent things as they never have been and never will be. . . .

There are different kinds of 'I-figures'. Tristram Shandy belongs to a familiar class of narrators – including Moll Flanders, Gulliver, Holden Caulfield, Huckleberry Finn – who claim to be someone entirely different from the author, and who tell their own personal history in an idiosyncratic manner. We could call these 'confessional' narrators. Being strongly dramatized, these fictitious narrators are volubly interpersonal, using the 'I' pronoun frequently, and constantly talking to the reader. A second type of narrator is classically illustrated by Conrad's Marlow, the 'story-teller' who is, like the confessional narrator, manifestly distinct from the author, but in this case focuses less on his own personal history and experiences than on some train of events which he happens to have witnessed. Somewhere in between the two types is a narrator like Fitzgerald's Nick Carraway who tells someone else's history in which he has been closely involved. In all cases of first-person narration, the I-figure can easily be treated ironically by the implied author: the narrator's voice may be self-betraying, or the implied author may intrude directly, as in the Marlow stories where Conrad's 'second self' intrudes obviously, busily setting the scene for the story-telling.

A different type of I-figure, in a more delicate relationship with the implied author, is the speaker who claims to be the *real author* and not some fictitious figure. Despite Swift's pretence, it is obvious that there is no Lemuel Gulliver, that 'Lemuel Gulliver' is a construct of a real author separate from his imaginary narrator. By contrast, there are narrators who as it were impersonate their creators: the genial and garrulous 'Fielding' of *Tom Jones*, the moral but compassionate 'George Eliot' of *The Mill on the Floss* and *Middlemarch*. 'Fielding' is fairly obviously a role, and much of his discourse is palpably ironic; with George Eliot, however, one is inclined to drop the quotation marks – the tone is sincere and in such a case the distinction between real author and implied author becomes more difficult to perceive.

Henry Fielding's 'Fielding'* is a most confidently dramatized 'authorial' presence, with an overt and loquacious relationship with the reader. He poses as a 'historian', asserting his independence from his narrative material, emphasizing his role as a selector and organizer; some-

* Terminology is difficult here. The quotation marks around 'Fielding' indicate the I-figure of the novel, who claims to be the author of the novel. Henry Fielding, unquoted, means Henry Fielding. Short of an absurd proliferation of quotation marks, there is little one can do about the ambiguity of pronouns. Unquoted He in the next sentence (and usually) means 'Fielding'.

times confessing to the limitations of his knowledge, sometimes professing privileged information; commenting both on the implications of the story and on his own method of handling it. The dominant style of *Tom Jones* (1749) is a blend of the essayistic and the argumentative, and is set by the introductory chapters to each of the eighteen books of the novel. Many of these are apologies or explanations for the compositional techniques of the novel, and they call attention to the controlling hand of the novelist and to his dependence on the reader's tolerance. Other introductory essays invite the reader's concurrence with 'Fielding's' prejudices against his favourite *bêtes noires* – philosophers, doctors, landladies. Interpersonal features of language (first and second person pronouns, questions, exclamations, etc.) are in evidence, though 'Fielding' tends to refer to the typical reader by the third person – 'the reader', 'the judicious reader', 'he' – in effect inviting the actual reader to compare himself with the ideal reader whom 'Fielding' addresses. The following paragraphs from the beginning of Ch. 1 of Bk. III are typical of 'Fielding's' dealings with the reader of *Tom Jones*:

The reader will be pleased to remember, that, at the beginning of the second book of this history, we gave him a hint of our intention to pass over several large periods of time, in which nothing happened worthy of being recorded in a chronicle of this kind.

In so doing, we do not only consult our own dignity and ease, but the good and advantage of the reader: for besides, that, by these means, we prevent him from throwing away his time, in reading without either pleasure or emolument, we give him, at all such seasons, an opportunity of employing that wonderful sagacity, of which he is master, by filling up these vacant spaces of time with his own conjectures; for which purpose, we have taken care to qualify him in the preceding pages.

For instance, what reader but knows that Mr All-worthy felt, at first, for the loss of his friend, those emotions of grief, which, on such occasions, enter into all men whose hearts are not composed of flint, or their heads of as solid materials? Again, what reader doth not know that philosophy and religion, in time, moderated, and at last extinguished this grief? The former of these, teaching the folly and vanity of it, and the latter, correcting it as unlawful; and at the same time assuaging it, by raising future hopes and assurances, which enable a strong and religious mind to take leave of a friend, on his death-bed, with little less indifference than if he was preparing for a long journey; and, indeed, with little less hope of seeing him again.

One of 'Fielding's' main aims in *Tom Jones* is to persuade the reader to accept the scheme of moral values which the implied author projects on the characters, i.e. to make the implied author's and reader's evaluative perspectives coincide; in this moral scheme, prudence is exalted over recklessness, generosity over self-interest.

'Fielding' doesn't hesitate to announce directly his views on the ethics of human behaviour, both by explicit comment (often sarcastic) on the actions of his characters, and by proclamations of general moral 'truths'. The latter may be announced in the form of aphoristic *generic sentences*. These are very recognizable semi-proverbial sentences in which the speaker asserts the truth of the predicate in respect of all possible referents of the subject noun phrase. Such sentences are typically cast in the 'timeless' present tense. As a simple example, 'Fielding' might say something like 'All innkeepers are rapacious' and claim by it that at any time and place, any innkeeper you meet will be set on cheating you out of your money. The generic sentence is a regular tell-tale of the intrusive, assertive, author. But the moralistic and authoritarian connotations of this form are so strong that Fielding and other novelists tend either to disguise it or to restrict the overt generalizing surface structure to ironic or facetious usages:

> As sympathies of all kinds are apt to beget love, so experience teaches us that none have a more direct tendency this way than those of a religious kind between persons of different sexes.
>
> (*Tom Jones*, Bk. I, Ch. 2)

> It is a truth universally acknowledged, that a single man in possession of a good fortune, must be in want of a wife.
>
> (Jane Austen, *Pride and Prejudice*, 1813)

To avoid the alienating dogmatism of the explicit form of the generic, novelists submit it to various transformational disguises so that it does not appear blatantly in the surface structure. The third paragraph of the longer extract from *Tom Jones* shows several ways in which generics may be transformed away from their dogmatic surface structures but still be cunningly asserted. The following general claims are made:

1 On such occasions emotions of grief enter into all men whose hearts are not composed of flint or whose heads are not composed of as solid materials.
2 Philosophy and religion in time moderate grief.
3 Philosophy and religion at last extinguish grief.
4 Philosophy teaches the folly and vanity of grief.
5 Religion corrects grief as unlawful.
6 Religion assuages grief.
7 Religion raises future hopes and assurances.
8 Future hopes and assurances enable a strong and religious mind to take leave of a friend.

and so on.

All of these generic assertions exist as full generalizing propositions in the deep structure of the text's sentences, but they have been transformationally disguised on the route to the surface. 1 has become a subordinate clause within a sentence which is ostensibly a question ('What reader but knows?' = 'Every reader knows') in the past tense ('felt'). 2 and 3 have been subjected to transformations: again, the apparent question and past tense are surface forms superficially at odds with the usual structure of generics, tempering the potential dogmatism. 4, 5, 6 and 7 have all been split up and distributed among separate sentences in the surface structure. Their subjects are cited in one sentence and then pronominalized ('the former . . . the latter') in the next, and then finally deleted (' . . . assuaging . . . raising'). The -*ing* form of the predicates allows the removal of the tell-tale 'timeless present'. 8 is fairly closely represented in its surface structure, retaining its present tense although downgraded to a relative clause, like 1.

The process of interpretation attributed to the reader in these paragraphs is craftily referred to as 'conjecture'. It is actually deduction from general premises allegedly shared by author and reader. Fielding suggests that 'Every reader knows that [generics 1–8]; apply these truths to a man of Mr Allworthy's character and situation, and you can deduce that he was at first sorrowful and after a while consoled'. The generalizations are enclosed within rhetorical questions to which the only appropriate answer is 'Yes'; and the affirmative commits the reader to acceptance of the consolations of philosophy and religion. Since the content of the disguised generic sentences is, viewed charitably, tendentious, and viewed realistically, vacuous, it is as well that they were not stated in the open form of my paraphrases 1–8. The overt generic surface structure is tantamount to saying 'I believe that . . .', 'I claim that . . .' and is vulnerable to sceptical challenge in a way that 'We know that . . .' appears not to be. The transformed version, presupposing the reader's agreement, exemplifies one of the devices by which the discourse of fiction encourages willing suspension of disbelief. It allows outspoken, sententious writers (Fielding and George Eliot are the most prominent examples in English) to moderate the style of their general claims to wisdom, to suggest that society, rather than the author personally, is responsible for the judgements he makes.

The author and his characters

We now turn to discourse relationships between the author – or his assumed self – and his characters. The novelist ultimately controls their actions, their thoughts, their speech, their appearance and all their other qualities; he knows everything about them. But in his presentation of his characters, he need not seem to be omniscient or omnipotent – he may or may not choose to appear as a knowing puppet-master. He has a number of options as to how much, and how, he reveals; to what extent he allows the characters' consciousnesses to be liberated from his own, and to what extent their thoughts are infiltrated and coloured by the quality of his own thoughts. These are, of course, linguistic options, so if we examine closely the narrative discourse we will find clues, in the choice of words and of syntactic constructions, as to how the creator of a prose fiction and his creatures 'stand' in relation to one another.

Internal and external views

A basic distinction may be drawn between 'internal' and 'external' perspectives on the thoughts and desires of characters. The *internal* view opens to us characters' states of mind, reactions and motives, either by narrative report (and judgement, inescapably), by the telling of what in real life would be hidden from an observer, or by one of the more dramatized, soliloquy-like, 'stream of consciousness' or 'interior monologue' techniques. The *external* perspective accepts

the privacy of other people's experience: the writer constructs, for himself and thus for us, the role of an unprivileged observer coming to partial understanding of the fictional figures in a fragmentary way. There are many variants
of compositional strategy and of language within each of
these alternatives, and I have space to review only some of
them.

Many novelists maintain a point of view consistently
either internal or external, because shifting from one mode
to the other draws attention to the artifice of the processes
involved and so to the technique of the writer. On the other
hand, mixing of modes characterizes some avant-garde
fiction, as well as older writings with strongly realized,
confident and voluble narrators. 'Fielding' usually reports
his characters' motives openly, but sometimes withdraws,
telling us that he doesn't know what is happening inside the
character's head. This sort of open modal switching is an
excellent source of examples for us, since we find internal
and external perspectives side by side in descriptions of the
same scene. Here, for instance, is a sequence from *The Mill
on the Floss* in which the narrator moves rapidly from one
type of discourse to its antithesis. Maggie, almost adult,
walks through an overgrown quarry and is intercepted by
Philip Wakem:

You may see her now, as she walks down the favourite
turning, and enters the Deeps by a narrow path through
a group of Scotch firs – her tall figure and old lavender-
gown visible through an hereditary black-silk shawl of
some wide-meshed net-like material; and now she is sure
of being unseen, she takes off her bonnet and ties it over
her arm. One would certainly suppose her to be farther
on in life than her seventeenth year – perhaps because of
the slow resigned sadness of the glance, from which all
search and unrest seem to have departed, perhaps because
her broad-chested figure has the mould of early woman-

hood. Youth and health have withstood well the in-
voluntary and voluntary hardships of her lot, and the
nights in which she has lain on the hard floor for a penance
have left no obvious trace; the eyes are liquid, the brown
cheek is firm and rounded, the full lips are red. With her
dark colouring and jet crown surmounting her tall figure,
she seems to have a sort of kinship with the grand Scotch
firs, at which she is looking up as if she loved them well.
Yet one has a sense of uneasiness in looking at her – a
sense of opposing elements, of which a fierce collision is
imminent: surely there is a hushed expression, such as one
often sees in older faces under borderless caps, out of keeping with the resistant youth, which one expects to flash
out in a sudden, passionate glance, that will dissipate all
the quietude, like a damped fire leaping out again when
all seemed safe.

But Maggie herself was not uneasy at this moment.
She was calmly enjoying the free air, while she looked up
at the old fir-trees, and thought that those broken ends
of branches were the records of past storms, which had
only made the red stems soar higher. But while her eyes
were still turned upward, she became conscious of a
moving shadow cast by the evening sun on the grassy
path before her, and looked down with a startled gesture
to see Philip Wakem, who first raised his hat, and then,
blushing deeply, came forward to her and put out his
hand. Maggie, too, coloured with surprise, which soon
gave way to pleasure. She put out her hand and looked
down at the deformed figure before her with frank eyes,
filled for the moment with nothing but the memory of her
child's feelings – a memory that was always strong in her.

The framework surrounding this passage is one of direct
discourse between narrator and reader. The first paragraph begins with the direct interpersonal address of 'you'
and a switch of tense into present, suggesting a community

of viewpoint between narrator and reader, external to Maggie. We interpret, make guesses about, her mental state as we spy on her in her walk; we speculate about how she feels, on the basis of how she looks. Many of the classic linguistic signs of a narrator deliberately situating herself outside the character's consciousness are found here: speculative verbs such as 'seem' (three times) and 'suppose', and adverbs and conjunctions which emphasize interpretation rather than factual report: 'certainly', 'perhaps', 'surely', 'as if'; comparisons citing known phenomena in order to make comprehensible a hidden inner state: 'such as', 'like'; expressions of tentativeness or indefiniteness: 'some', 'a sense of', 'a sort of'. Words and phrases like these, in this kind of discourse context, are called *words of estrangement*. 'Expressions of this type occur in the text when the narrator takes an external point of view in describing some internal state (thoughts, feelings, unconscious motives for an action) that he cannot be sure about' (Boris Uspensky, see p. 138 below). For fiction, one would qualify this definition somewhat: the novelist can always be sure about any state which he attributes to his characters, since he is absolutely in control of their feelings. So an estranged discourse is chosen for a particular reason: it is a discourse pose which the author attributes to his narrator when he has some aesthetic reason for pretending innocence or distance.

The next paragraph shifts into the opposite modality, offering a confident presentation of the feelings of the heroine. The inner view is signalled linguistically by the appearance of a class of state predicates called *verba sentiendi*, 'words of feeling', expressions denoting mental states, emotions, acts of thought. They designate unobservables of consciousness which in real life are accessible only if the subject reports them. 'Not uneasy', 'calmly', 'enjoying', 'thought that', 'conscious', 'surprise', 'pleasure', 'memory', 'feelings'. Maggie's sensitivity and responsiveness, and her high degree of emotional agitation, are made evident and to some extent analysed. This is not, of course, stream of consciousness technique, despite its psychological explicitness. The narrator reports the contents of Maggie's mind, but she does not shape the syntax to mimic the way Maggie's thoughts are articulated, nor does she make any attempt to erase her own presence as a reporter, to suggest that Maggie's thoughts are witnessed by us directly without intervention. The stream of consciousness method of Joyce, or Woolf, or Faulkner, seeks to give the illusion of directness by suppressing the author and by miming the associative flux of pre-verbal thought. George Eliot intends nothing of this kind. The first paragraph places the reader in the position of an unprivileged external observer, and emphasizes the speculative quality of our assessments of other people. The movement to an internal view, with the very authoritarian announcement at the start of the next paragraph, takes us from speculation to certitude (from *our* speculation to the narrator's, and implicitly the author's, certitude). We remain extremely conscious of the tone of the novelist, even though the subject of the paragraph is Maggie's feelings. So in this context, the internal view communicates the narrative discourse stance, as well as the character's thoughts: describing Maggie, at the same time it contributes to the characterization of 'George Eliot'.

External perspective

External perspective, marked by its 'words of estrangement', may be adopted for a variety of different reasons. The most elementary case would be depiction of an unknown figure seen at a distance or behaving puzzlingly: the observer is forced to guess at what moves the character, what clues to personality can be gleaned from the indistinct façade of appearance. Or, a person who is regarded as essentially enigmatic may have his air of mystery conveyed by the technique of estrangement. A step further, and externality leads to alienation, the creation of an inhuman gap between the observer and the character: the character is incomprehensible, unreachable, scarcely a member of the human race. Dickens's grotesque villains are sometimes treated in this way; here is Bounderby from *Hard Times*:

He was a rich man: banker, merchant, manufacturer, and what not. A big, loud man, with a stare, and a metallic laugh. A man made out of a coarse material, which seemed to have been stretched to make so much of him. A man with a great puffed head and forehead, swelled veins in his temples, and such a strained skin to his face that it seemed to hold his eyes open, and lift his eyebrows up. A man with a pervading appearance on him of being inflated like a balloon, and ready to start. A man who could never sufficiently vaunt himself a self-made man. A man who was always proclaiming, through that brassy speaking-trumpet of a voice of his, his old ignorance and his old poverty. A man who was the Bully of humility.

A year or two younger than his eminently practical friend, Mr Bounderby looked older; his seven or eight and forty might have had seven or eight added to it again, without surprising anybody. He had not much hair. One might have fancied he had talked it off; and that what was left, all standing up in disorder, was in that condition from being constantly blown about by his windy boastfulness.

We have here the familiar modal signs of estrangement: 'seemed' twice, 'appearance', 'looked', 'might have had', 'might have fancied'. Struggling to grasp Bounderby's essence from his external appearance, Dickens evolves a series of bizarre but consistent comparisons – images of wind inflating Bounderby like a balloon, ready to propel him on, bursting from him when he speaks. These images derive from a conventional psychological metaphor (wind

= boastfulness), but that isn't their sole point; they also diagram Bounderby as a perplexing and threatening *object* or *force* which intrudes menacingly into 'our' more human world.

The above passage exhibits a remarkably severe and potent distancing, an utter dissociation of the author from his character. But there are less alienating uses of external perspective. Often it signifies respect for the mental privacy of characters, and acknowledgement that our assessments of people are limited, conjectural. Used in this way, external perspective is one of the conventions of 'realism' (as it so patently is not in Dickens): it reproduces the gradual and fragmentary fashion in which we come to any knowledge of the people we encounter. The writer carefully conceals his own omniscience, releasing information about his characters only a little at a time, tentatively, being sparing with judgements, as if the narrator and the reader have no unnatural advantage of insight or foreknowledge over an ordinary inquisitive observer.

The opening pages of Henry James's *The Portrait of a Lady* (1881) illustrate well this slow process of revelation, presented as if it were deduction from externals. Ralph Touchett, his father, and Lord Warburton are taking tea on the lawn one late summer afternoon. They are introduced in the vaguest terms: 'Those [people] that I have in mind', 'The persons concerned', 'an old man', 'two younger men', 'The old man', 'His companions', 'One of them', 'the elder man'. Their first appearance is visual, distant and insubstantial: we see them as shadows: 'The shadows on the perfect lawn were straight and angular; they were the shadows of an old man . . . and of two younger men.' We infer that the old man is the owner of the ancient country house which stages this scene; there is a digression on the history of the house and on its architecture and setting, then the narrator returns us to the three men, this time presenting visual close-ups interspersed with fragments of background information. The dominant tone of the discourse is one of cautious hypothesis; this tone arises largely from the linguistic features italicized in the following extract:

The old gentleman at the tea-table, who had come from America thirty years before, had brought with him, at the top of his baggage, his American *physiognomy*; and he had not only brought it with him, but he had kept it in the best order, so that, if necessary, he might have taken it back to his own country with perfect confidence. At present, *obviously*, nevertheless, he was *not likely* to displace himself; his journeys were over and he was taking the rest that precedes the great rest. He had a narrow, clean-shaven face, with features evenly distributed and an *expression* of placid acuteness. It was *evidently* a face in which the range of representation was not large, so that the *air* of contented shrewdness was all the more of a merit. It *seemed to tell* that he had been successful in life, yet it *seemed to tell* also that his success had not been exclusive and invidious, but had had much of the inoffensiveness of failure. He had *certainly* had a great experience of men, but there was *an almost rustic simplicity* in the faint smile that played upon his lean, spacious cheek and lighted up his humorous eye as he at last slowly and carefully deposited his big tea-cup upon the table. . . .

One of these [other gentlemen] was a remarkably well-made man of five-and-thirty, with a *face* as English as that of the old gentleman I have just sketched was something else; a *noticeably* handsome face, fresh-coloured, fair and frank, with firm, straight features, a lively grey eye and the rich adornment of a chestnut beard. This person had *a certain* fortunate, brilliant exceptional *look* – the *air* of a happy temperament fertilised by a high civilisation – which would have made almost any *observer* envy him at a venture. He was booted and spurred, *as if* he had dismounted from a long ride; he wore a white hat, which *looked* too large for him. . . .

The narrator and the reader share the position of 'observer', standing well outside the characters and scrutinizing physical details of face, dress and posture. The activity of interpretation is emphasized by the transformation of eye, cheek and face into general terms of appearance: 'physiognomy', 'expression', 'air', 'look' begin to sum up the suggestions of, or impressions made by, the physical features. There are plenty of modal adverbs and adjectives – 'obviously', 'evidently', 'a certain', etc. – which, however confident in their assertion, in effect draw attention to the speculative quality of the judgements. It is a commonplace that the word 'certain' in James means exactly its opposite, and the reason for this semantic reversal emerges when it is seen as part of a pervasive pattern of tentative modalization, in which the observer places himself and us in an estranged position from which we can only guess at what the characters' features 'seem' to tell.

Internal perspective

Just as external perspective may or may not be a convention for 'realistic' representation, depending on how it is handled, so a similar choice of functions is available within *internal* perspective. At one extreme, in the second paragraph of the extract from *The Mill on the Floss* quoted above, we have Maggie's sensations reported in a style which is uncompromisingly 'author's language': the thoughts of a seventeen-year-old girl are given in a style indistinguishable from the mature, philosophical voice of the author. No attempt is made to dramatize Maggie as a separate individual, or to catch the exact quality of her thoughts at this particular moment of emotional crisis. At the other extreme, we have the 'psychological realism' of Joycean stream-of-consciousness where, instead of subordinating the character to his

own voice, the narrator effaces himself to release the character as an independent subject expressing the special nature
of his mental experience; Leopold Bloom in the following
sentences indulges in psychological associations with what
he sees out of the window of a carriage, and Joyce produces
a style wholly adjusted to conveying the content and structure of that mental experience:

> The carriage halted short.
> – What's wrong?
> – We're stopped.
> – Where are we?
> Mr Bloom put his head out of the window.
> – The grand canal, he said.
> Gasworks. Whooping cough they say it cures. Good
> job Milly never got it. Poor children! Doubles them up
> black and blue with convulsions. Shame really. Got off
> lightly with illness compared. Only measles. Flaxseed tea.
> Scarlatina, influenza epidemics. Canvassing for death.
> Don't miss this chance. Dogs' home over there. Poor old
> Athos! Be good to Athos, Leopold, is my last wish. Thy
> will be done. We obey them in the grave. A dying scrawl.
> He took it to heart, pined away. Quiet brute. Old men's
> dogs usually are.
> A raindrop spat on his hat. He drew back and saw an
> instant of shower spray dots over the grey flags. Apart.
> Curious. Like through a colander. I thought it would.
> My boots were creaking I remember now.
> The weather is changing, he said quietly.
>
> (*Ulysses*, 1922)

This use of language to mime the structure of the character's
thoughts illustrates an extreme of personal discourse com-
pared with George Eliot (who allows Maggie no personal
mind-style), and a different theory of realism contrasted
with James, for Joyce proposes that individuals can be
intimately known and shown.

Note that 'realism' is not an actuality, but a convention, a theory. Henry James in *The Portrait of a Lady*, or in his more withdrawn way Hemingway in *The Killers*, writes to a theory of the way people have knowledge of each other; Joyce articulates the thoughts of Leopold Bloom in an artificially constructed language which, by convention, has come to be accepted as the representation of a fragmented, unfocused consciousness of that sort. Whether or not this language 'accurately' represents some psychological process is an unanswerable question, for our experience of the Bloom thought-process is derived entirely from the language, and no language-independent level of thought can be discovered. We can't compare the *object* and the *medium* of representation, can't ask whether Joyce's language accurately represents Bloom's consciousness, because the object doesn't exist separate from the medium. 'Realism' is a convention of discourse; or rather, several conventions, since a range of different patternings give rise to the impression of realism in different writers and different works.

Within the conventions of internal perspective, an author may or may not give an impression of the texture of his characters' thoughts; and as the discourse expresses their consciousness, it may be sympathetic or it may be critical. Some of the possibilities may be illustrated by a few short extracts. The first, from Thackeray's *Vanity Fair* (1848), is a commentary on the isolation of Amelia Sedley in the crisis of the bankruptcy of her father and her desertion by George Osborne:

The father had forgotten the poor girl. She was lying, awake and unhappy, overhead. In the midst of friends, home, and kind parents, she was alone. To how many people can one tell all? Who will be open when there is no sympathy, or has call to speak to those who never can understand? Our gentle Amelia was thus solitary. She had no confidante, so to speak, ever since she had anything

> to confide. She could not tell the old mother her doubts
> and cares; the would-be sisters seemed every day more
> strange to her. And she had misgivings and fears which
> she dared not acknowledge to herself, though she was
> always secretly brooding over them.

Her feelings are confidently labelled, categorized: 'unhappy',
'solitary', 'doubts', 'cares', 'misgivings', 'fears', 'brooding'.
But though these are inner-view, psychological, terms, they
are general and shallow, as if the narrator isn't really interested in analysing the girl's sorrows in their specificity.
Nor does the language convey any hint of how Amelia
herself might articulate her grief while reflecting on her misfortune: the style is not personal or expressive. The foreign-
ness of phrases like 'our gentle Amelia', 'the old mother',
'the would-be sisters' and (in the next paragraph) 'the
poor little martyr' to any mode of thinking which might be
Amelia's own brings home the fact that, despite the list
of feelings given in internal perspective, the discourse is
totally the story-teller's own. This is not sympathetic psychological analysis, but the puppet-master's *judgement* on
the poor little martyr.

Judgement may be passed even in internal discourse
which *does* express the style of the character's mind. The
best known and most spectacular instance is *A Portrait of the
Artist as a Young Man* (which is third person narration and
not interior monologue), in which Joyce continuously provides new styles to match and dramatize the stages of his
hero's intellectual and spiritual development. The language
is always obviously Stephen's and not the narrator's or the
implied author's; the continuous dramatization of the
hero's mind – as baby, schoolboy, adolescent – implies
the suppression of the narrating voice, and behind that, the
dissociation of authorial values. The *Portrait* is luxuriantly
internal, but ironic.

There is a simpler case of irony in my next extract, which

I have chosen to set beside *Vanity Fair*; it is from Kingsley Amis's *Take a Girl like You* (1960), and like the Thackeray piece it enters a young girl's mind. Like Thackeray, Amis is unsympathetic; unlike him, but like Joyce, he gives the impression of reproducing his subject's style and thus communicates his distance by dramatic irony. In this passage Jenny Bunn, an ignorant provincial virgin come South, reviews the evening she has just spent at a pretentious 'roadhouse' with a prospective boyfriend:

A peep in the glass showed her that the red wool sheath dress, though not new, was doing its job, making the best of her bust without being too ostentatious, and the back-swept hair with medium earrings gave the right sort of grown-up look. And she had got through the restaurant part quite decently, asking Patrick to do the choosing for her – a good tip from *Woman's Domain* – and getting rid of nearly all the raw fish and sort of meat fritter and rather sharp wine without hankering much after a gravy dinner and a cider. She had managed the cutlery all right, too, by just keeping her head and working inwards from the outside. And it was so smashing here: not only the curly iron fences but the bar downstairs, with the waiter coming over specially to light her cigarette and emptying the ashtray every few minutes; and then all the business in the restaurant, with the foreign-accented waiter bringing the bottle of wine to show Patrick (who had said approvingly 'Nice and full') before it was opened. No doubt there was a ballroom somewhere in the building, where they had big dances at the weekends, probably with bands like Johnny Dankworth's or Humphrey Lyttelton's. The whole thing made her feel treasured and – something she would have died rather than admit to anyone but Trixie – like a starlet or a singer.

The language in which Jenny's perceptions and reflections

are couched is pointedly Jenny's, not narrator's or the implied author's. Her thoughts are being transcribed more or less directly. One reliable sign of this is the structure of the sentence 'And it was so smashing here' which is cast in what is called *free indirect style*, a mode in which thought or speech is only partly rephrased to fit the past tense of the narration. Compare:

Direct: (1) She thought 'And it is so smashing here'.
Free indirect: (2) And it was so smashing here.
Indirect: (3) She thought how smashing it was there.

The distinctive feature of (2) is the combination of a past-tense verb with a present-tense adverb * 'here'; (1) (within the quotation marks) is consistently present, (3) consistently past. 'Here' can only signal Jenny's point of view; from the author's, she is 'there', not 'here'. In the context of 'was', 'here' noticeably asserts the replacement of the narrator's viewpoint by Jenny's. The vocabulary also is clearly her own. 'Smashing', 'treasured', 'would have died', 'starlet' connote a 1950s sentimental adolescent drawing her terms secondhand from the popular media of the time (cf. the frequent contemptuous references to '*Woman's Domain*'). Jenny has moved into a culture whose signs and meanings she finds hard to interpret: 'Some of the . . . things in the room were easy to understand . . . Other things were less straightforward . . .' When, so often, she doesn't know what things

---

* Calling an adverb of *place* 'present tense' abbreviates, I hope not too confusingly, a complicated argument about the way language analyses space and time. Both space and time are patterned on the opposition 'proximate' versus 'non-proximate', categories seen in relation to the space-time point of utterance. 'Proximate' words include *is, now, here, this*; 'non-proximate', *was, then, there, that*. The combination of past tense (non-proximate) with the proximate temporal adverb *now* is the commonest indicator of free indirect style, found scores of times in Amis's novel, e.g. the sentence immediately preceding our extract: 'Jenny decid*ed* that, in spite of the rather funny atmosphere of the last ten minutes, things *had* gone pretty well up to *now*.'

are, she reveals her ignorance by not knowing what they are *called*: 'raw fish and sort of meat fritter', 'the remains of the huge pink fish'. Nervously self-conscious about her own naïveté, she relies on proxies to categorize her experience, and so her thoughts are an incongruous patchwork of scraps of phrases culled from women's magazines, teenage culture and banal sayings of her father's. By making his narrator quote Jenny directly rather than paraphrase and interpret her thoughts, Amis allows her to condemn herself – her second-hand language, which he handles with distaste, is far removed from author's language, and the values it encodes are far from those of the author.

Discourse structure and mind-style

We may coin the term 'mind-style' to refer to any distinctive linguistic presentation of an individual mental self. A mind-style may analyse a character's mental life more or less radically; may be concerned with relatively superficial or relatively fundamental aspects of the mind; may seek to dramatize the order and structure of conscious thoughts, or just present the topics on which a character reflects, or display preoccupations, prejudices, perspectives and values which strongly bias a character's world-view but of which s/he may be quite unaware. These different discourse structures call upon a variety of linguistic techniques for their expression. Consider Jenny Bunn's mind-style. Amis intends only a relatively shallow analysis of her mentality: his narrator's scorn is directed at the poverty of *content* of her mind rather than at the structure of her thoughts. He can therefore achieve the characterization at the superficial linguistic level of vocabulary and phraseology, by attributing to Jenny choices of words, idioms and clichés which betray the limitations of her experience and social affiliations. On the other hand, syntax as well as vocabulary is important in establishing Leopold Bloom's mind-style. The words he uses convey an impression of sentimental vulgarity, and mark his scatter-brained flitting from topic to topic. But the syntax of his mind-style is especially striking. The obviously dominant features of the surface structure are the brevity of his sentences and the constant transformational deletion of parts of their deep structures. An elliptic, allusive privacy results; also, a style of thought which, through lack of syntactic elaboration, is incapable of any exploratory, analytic, development of an idea. Complex sentences combining numbers of deep structures in a variety of ways – a syntax absolutely avoided in Joyce's handling of Bloom's thoughts – suggest, rightly or wrongly, logical sophistication, precision, mental flexibility; Bloom's syntax connotes crudeness, dogmatism, lack of intellectual finesse.

In stream-of-consciousness writers such as Joyce, Faulkner, Proust or Virginia Woolf, surface structure syntax is used to dramatize the structure of characters' and narrators' conscious thoughts, different syntaxes resulting in different impressions of the flow of thought. There is in fact also a range of much more radical modes of analysis of characters' psyches, depending on the novelist's choice of structures at deeper levels of linguistic form. By assigning a consistent type of semantic structure to a character, or managing some particularly significant transformations in a distinctive way, the novelist is able to convey not only the sequence of a character's thoughts – whether he progresses jerkily and illogically like Bloom, or fluently and associatively like Mrs Woolf's heroines, and so on – but also the implicit structure and quality of his outlook on the world. There is an excellent demonstration of this by the linguist M. A. K. Halliday in his analysis * of William Golding's presentation of the mind of Neanderthal man in *The Inheritors*. By attention to what I have called discourse structure, Halliday reveals how the cognitive limitations of primitive man are linguistically conveyed. In the passage analysed, the Neanderthaler

* 'Linguistic function and literary style,' see p. 137 below.

Lok watches, without comprehending, an adversary from a
more advanced tribe drawing a bow and shooting an arrow
at him:

> The bushes twitched again. Lok steadied by the tree
> and gazed. A head and a chest faced him, half-hidden.
> There were white bone things behind the leaves and hair.
> The man had white bone things above his eyes and under
> the mouth so that his face was longer than a face should
> be. The man turned sideways in the bushes and looked at
> Lok along his shoulder. A stick rose upright and there was
> a lump of bone in the middle. Lok peered at the stick and
> the lump of bone and the small eyes in the bone things
> over the face. Suddenly Lok understood that the man
> was holding the stick out to him but neither he nor Lok
> could reach across the river. He would have laughed if it
> were not for the echo of the screaming in his head. The
> stick began to grow shorter at both ends. Then it shot out
> to full length again.
>
> The dead tree by Lok's ear acquired a voice.
> 'Clop!'
> His ears twitched and he turned to the tree.

Halliday (commenting on an extract about twice as long
as this) points out that, although the language describes
Lok perceiving a sequence of actions, these actions are per-
ceived in a way which signifies a weak grasp of the power of
human beings to *control* the activity of the world around
them: 'The picture is one in which people act, but they do
not act on things; they move, but they move only themselves,
not other objects.' It is a world-view which might have
been held by pre-technological man, man innocent of his
innate ability to manipulate his environment and other
human beings. This perception is conveyed in a mind-style
consistently restricted by a choice of some basic structures
and avoidance of others. There is a particular lack of transitive clauses (Subject + Verb + Object) with human

subjects ('His enemy rustled the bushes' would be inappropriate to this style), i.e. clauses where a human agent brings about a change in some object or human patient other than himself. In Lok's universe, 'The bushes twitched again' – an inanimate object appears to move of its own accord when it has actually been shifted by a person; compare 'A stick rose upright', 'The stick began to grow shorter at both ends', 'The dead tree by Lok's ear acquired a voice'. When human agents are subjects, they are generally subjects of intransitives (Subject + Verb) – 'Lok . . . gazed' – which usually have the force of reflexives and/or relate to movement in a stated location: 'Lok steadied [himself] by the tree', 'The man turned [himself] sideways'. These constructions, adding up to a consistent restriction on syntactic patterning, imply a fundamental limitation of Lok's grasp of how the world works: he does not understand the relationship of *causation* – does not realize that a state of affairs can be brought about or changed by people's conscious will and action. Lok's failure to distinguish animate from inanimate objects (people and bushes seem to share the same powers of motion) is a related limitation: no special status is granted to people as agents. These conceptual deficiencies might be characteristic of a technologically primitive phase of humanity, and Halliday interprets the conquest of Lok and his group by the more advanced new people in these terms.

Agency and animacy are fundamental aspects of linguistic structure which are highly significant determiners of what I have called mind-style; they feature in a wide range of varieties of stylistic organization (not only Lok-styles!) and should always be examined in any study of discourse. I have space for only one more example of these processes, and for it I return to sentences 12–21 of the passage from David Storey's *Radcliffe*, discussed above with reference to textual structure and to visual perspective (pp. 57–61, 74–5 above).

12 The field disappeared through the fringe of trees.

13 Leonard sat stiffly, swaying with the truck, his gaze fixed on the scene behind. 14 For a while he could see the castle silhouetted several miles away, marking the spot; then the heavier, smoother shoulders of the lower valley rose up. 15 The road dropped suddenly and they ran between the first bands of stone terraces. 16 The green and white strands vanished, and the brown shadow of the valley bottom closed over the line of speeding trucks.

17 Houses, perched on the rocky outcrops, clung to the terraced edge of the moors. 18 Somewhere, running among them, was the river; its smell came into the truck as they followed its hidden course. 19 Then they rose into the sun again, the valley cleared below and the river flowed through a narrow strip of woods and over a ridge of shallow falls. 20 They rode with it for some time, then swept down again, the country levelling out. 21 The strings of houses enveloped the valley, first one side then the other, growing into a broader elongation of brick and stone, thickening, deepening, then darkening.

Remember that the text presents, not what Leonard thinks but what he sees as he looks from the moving truck; now the *way* he perceives is analysed by the language. Leonard is a fragile, hypersensitive, tormented young man for whom the world around him, both people and places, is oppressive and threatening. *Radcliffe* is a modern 'Gothic' novel, deliberately following the conventions which were set by such early pioneers as Horace Walpole's *Castle of Otranto* (1765), Anne Radcliffe's *Mysteries of Udolpho* (1794) and Mary Shelley's *Frankenstein* (1817) and developed by numbers of writers of popular horror fiction and romantic fiction through the nineteenth and twentieth centuries. One major convention relates the characters to the settings in which their psychological fantasies are played: settings are hostile, mysterious, portentous, felt by the protagonists to have their own power to menace and harm. In part, this convention is achieved by providing a scenic backdrop of ruins, the gloomier type of picturesque landscape, storms and the like, on which the characters can ruminate. These settings may be more or less animated, endowed with the power to influence and act upon people.

Leonard certainly feels that his surroundings assail him with malicious violence. The most dramatic manifestation is the desolate house, 'like an animal crouched at the summit of the hill', in which he lives, and which shakes and thunders as if to destroy him. But this threat is generalized, continuously present in the language of Leonard's vision. In the extract, two features of discourse contribute to this impression. First, the simple fact that the subjects of many sentences are names for parts of the landscape: 'The field disappeared' (12), 'The road dropped' (15), 'Houses . . . clung to . . .' (17), 'the river flowed' (19), etc. We ordinarily talk about rivers flowing, so in itself such an expression is quite unexceptional. It is the consistency with which this sort of construction is chosen (where alternatives are possible) that makes the point. What actually happens when 'the field disappeared' is not a movement on the part of the field but a change in Leonard's viewpoint so that he can no longer see the field: but the placing of 'the field' in the position of syntactic surface subject suggests that the field *did something* – moved of its own accord – in this context where inanimate objects frequently occupy this syntactic position.

Leonard's impression of the activeness of the landscape, suggested by this simple syntactic device, is reinforced by the semantic juxtapositions of the noun phrases denoting parts of the landscape and the verbs accompanying and energizing them. Verbs which usually take animate subjects are linked with inanimates. The houses 'perch' and 'cling', taking on the attributes of birds; the valley has 'shoulders' which rise up menacingly; 'close over' and 'envelop' are two more active predicates assigned to aspects of the scene. It is these discourse structures, related to 'personification' in traditional metaphorical terms, which make us feel through Leonard's perception a sense of closure, constriction, threat. The effect might be put down to 'atmosphere', but it is an atmosphere which the discourse attributes to Leonard's way of presenting the world to himself.

My next example of language analysing the structure of consciousness is taken from a very different writer, and involves transformational structure. In his later novels, Henry James develops an extreme technique of internal perspective: the novels are constructed so that the whole of their represented world is filtered through the vision of one central character, who thus becomes both subject and viewpoint simultaneously. Such a bifocal arrangement is comprehensible in terms of the present theory of discourse. A third person narrator deliberately restricts what he tells us to what the character has experienced, and relates the experiences in a style which displays the quality of the character's engagement with the world. (A difficulty with James's writing is that his heroes are so consistently and thoroughly afflicted with the mind-style in question that we begin to suspect it is James's own.) A sentence from *The Ambassadors* was quoted earlier for difficulty of syntactic processing (p. 9). If we put it in its context, we see that it exhibits transformational patterns which, repeated in the surrounding text, quickly imply a distinctive habit of thought:

1 She had, this lady, a perfect plain propriety, an expensive subdued suitability, that her companion was not free to analyse, but that struck him, so that his consciousness of it was instantly acute, as a quality quite new to him. 2 Before reaching her he stopped on the grass and went through the form of feeling for something, possibly forgotten, in the light overcoat he carried on his arm; yet the essence of the act was no more than the impulse to

gain time. 3 Nothing could have been odder than Strether's sense of himself as at that moment launched in something of which the sense would be quite disconnected from the sense of his past and which was literally beginning there and then. 4 It had begun in fact already upstairs and before the dressing-glass that struck him as blocking further, so strangely, the dimness of the window of his dull bedroom; begun with a sharper survey of the elements of Appearance than he had for a long time been moved to make. 5 He had during those moments felt these elements to be not so much to his hand as he should have liked, and then had fallen back on the thought that they were precisely a matter as to which help was supposed to come from what he was about to do. 6 He was about to go up to London, so that hat and necktie might wait. 7 What had come as straight to him as a ball in a well-played game – and caught moreover not less neatly – was just the air, in the person of his friend, of having seen and chosen, the air of achieved possession of those vague qualities and quantities that collectively figured to him as the advantage snatched from lucky chances. 8 Without pomp or circumstance, certainly, as her original address to him, equally with his own response, had been, he would have sketched to himself his impression of her as: 'Well, she's more thoroughly civilized —!' 9 If 'More thoroughly than *whom*?' would not have been for him a sequel to this remark, that was just by reason of his deep consciousness of the bearing of his comparison.

Like Jenny Bunn, Lambert Strether is an innocent abroad. A middle-aged man of limited experience, he has been sent from America to bring home the wayward Chad Newsome from Paris. At Chester, on his way to France, he meets worldly-wise Maria Gostrey; in the extract, he considers the impression she makes on him, ending with a half-suppressed comparison between her and his patroness Mrs Newsome.

Strether's response to the ways of Europe is circumspect and tentative. He doesn't explore his new milieu actively, but rather maintains himself in a receptive frame of mind open to impressions – which he reflects on in an exquisitely qualified manner. To call him 'passive' would be appropriate but inexact; the precise nature of this passivity needs specifying.

He hardly acts, physically (sentence 2 only), and his thought processes, though fertile and highly articulated, are almost never expressed as mental *actions* – that is, with Strether playing the role of agent of an action verb: 'He had felt' in sentence 5 only. Typically, any potential action predicates and state predicates which are attached to Strether are nominalized, as, for instance, in the final sentence 9: 'sequel', 'remark', 'consciousness', 'bearing', 'comparison'. Some of these nominalizations are transformations of predicates which might have been realized as verbs – 'he remarked' $\rightarrow$ 'his remark' – while others are nominalizations away from adjectives: 'he was conscious' $\rightarrow$ 'his consciousness'. The substitution of nouns for action verbs, found throughout this passage, is a standard convention in discourse contexts like this, and has obvious connotations of inactivity, repression of the agency function, reduction in the strength of the will in those human characters to whom this style is applied.

Nominalization of adjectives or state predicates contributes to this effect, but also has further implications. The boundary between description of state and passing of judgement is a tenuous one: compare 'She is sad' and 'She is vicious': isn't the former almost as much of a judgement as the latter? The construction 'Noun $+$ is $+$ Adjective' is the regular form for expressing judgements; a state predicate is attached to an individual, and the claim is made that the state designated by the predicate is a permanent quality of that individual. Now Strether is involved in the twofold evaluation of weighing up his new companion and comprehending his own responses; and it is noteworthy that, except in the hesitant and incomplete judgement of sentences 8–9, he avoids this adjectival structure. This is surely a significant evasion. Feelings, states, responses, whether his own or Maria Gostrey's, are given in non-judgemental form. Nominalization allows emotions and qualities to be presented as *possessions* which can be discarded, passed from person to person, traded, manipulated, etc.: non-inherent, not demanding commitment.

The first sentence is absolutely typical: the lady has 'a propriety', 'a suitability', 'a quality' as she might have an umbrella or a pet dog. As for Strether, he is debarred from any transitive relation to these qualities; 'was not free to analyse' (an obscure phrase which may be invoking ignorance or etiquette, but *syntactically* suggests that there is some external restraint upon Strether – he is not *allowed to* analyse). So he is unable to use adjectives analytically: he cannot think 'She is a perfectly proper lady'. Her objectified properties reach him only through a nominalized state of his own, 'his consciousness' (sentence 1). In this tortuous perceptual–evaluative process, Strether of course occupies the grammatical role of *patient*: 'struck him', 'quite new to him'. It is as if his feelings are disconnected from his own psyche; as if his perceptions assail him from outside, beyond his control; as if he relates to others and himself only through intermediaries; and it seems that he pictures others as suffering the same divided self. The three times repeated nominalization 'sense' in 3 draws attention to this process of mediation: through this term he relates to his present self, his present circumstances ('something') and his past experience. 'Sense', to which Strether relates as either possessor or patient, deprives him of the power of direct, active perception. These reified feelings – experienced as if they were independent objects – assail and bewilder him. In this context, the reader can be forgiven for momentarily misinterpreting 'the dressing-glass struck him' (4) literally, physically: Strether, not unlike Lok, inhabits a grotesque world in which inanimate objects are capable of rising up and assaulting one. The metaphor of the ball in the already-quoted sentence 7 is perfectly appropriate to this alienated psychic universe in which perception, feeling and personal attributes are shifted outside the subject's active control and away from the centre of his personality, transformed into missiles which the hostile world lobs at the helpless subject.

There is a physical parallel to the Jamesian nominalizations of psychological alienation in Lawrence's treatment of alienated sex, e.g. in *Sons and Lovers* (1913). This consists of making parts of the body perform sexual actions in a dissociated way, seemingly beyond the control of the lover and not needing his personal involvement. In Paul and Miriam's inhibited first love-making we find – among many active sentences where, it must be conceded, Paul behaves in a more integrated way – phrases such as 'his mouth was kissing her throat', 'his arms folded her closer and closer', 'his fingers wandered over her face', 'his mouth was on her throat'.

Conventions of discourse: Sociolinguistic structure in fiction

Sons and Lovers allows me to illustrate one further important fact about discourse and the novel. We have already seen how clusters of linguistic features – in the above extracts animacy, transitivity, agency, nominalization, passivization – are recurrently significant in a range of novels that are in other ways stylistically dissimilar. Discourse structure is, then, not idiosyncratic, not organized uniquely for each individual novel, but *conventional*. Structural patterns in a language by convention encode various interpersonal and cognitive experiences and relationships: the community has these expressive potentials generally available in the structure of its language, and the individual user of language chooses from them according to his personality, roles and communicative needs. (His 'choice' is by no means entirely conscious; many linguistic patterns follow automatically from the purpose, context and medium of communication, and some patterns may be unavailable for some types of writer.) Types and stages in the development of the novel manifest different structural selections from the universe of available discourse; different novelists have their individual styles of writing – we can parody them – but it would not be true to say that they create their personal languages out of a vacuum, for even the creative, conscious artist in written language is influenced and limited by what is available in the language at large. So we should not be surprised to find that some kinds of discourse structure which linguists find interesting in non-literary situations have their significances in novels too.

An obvious case to examine would be the treatment of speech, dialogue, in novels. 'Ordinary' conversational language has its rules of structure: e.g. dialect and accent are recognizable through regular features of a person's speech; and in conversation, different people's contributions are linked to each other, by various cohesive devices, into an integrated communicative whole. These conventional regularities of structure, non-literary in origin, may be as it were 'transcribed' out of real life into written fiction. Though the novelist performs a further stage of conventionalization in this transformation from speech to writing, we have here nevertheless a clear instance of structural overlap between two distinct situations of discourse, the language of life and the language of fiction. I simply cite this as an example of such overlap; the treatment of speech in the novel has been discussed elsewhere.*

* Norman Page, *Speech in the English Novel* (London: Longman, 1973).

Social structure in fictional discourse: elaborated and restricted codes

Of greater interest to us than, say, the representation of conversation or of dialect speech, would be some kind of linguistic variety with clear values associated with it in society at large, and utilized in fiction as a structuring device. Just such a device may be the distinction between 'restricted code' and 'elaborated code' proposed by the sociologist Basil Bernstein.* Bernstein suggests that the social class into which a speaker is born, through its influence on the structure of the family, determines the variety of English available to the child. If he is born into a working-class family, he will have access only to a 'restricted' variety of English, whereas the child of middle or upper class parents will additionally come to possess an 'elaborated' version of the language. (The blatantly evaluative connotations of the words 'restricted' and 'elaborated' are generally felt to be very unfortunate, but no agreed replacements have emerged so one may as well keep Bernstein's terms.)

The two codes are said to be learned not just through exposure to the prevailing modes of discourse within the two types of family, but also as a result of the roles and the kinds of behaviour and relationship found typically in the

* Basil Bernstein, *Class, Codes and Control* Vol I (London: Routledge and Kegan Paul, 1971). It must be admitted that Bernstein's theory is, empirically, rather weak; but I do not think this weakness affects the present discussion. Bernstein formulated his distinction between elaborated and restricted codes without reference to an adequate linguistic apparatus for describing the differences between them, and it has not been convincingly shown that working class and middle class sub-populations *actually* speak differently, as a general rule, in the way Bernstein claims they do. Indeed, it seems quite likely that the theory is basically the projection of divisive middle class prejudices on to a much more complicated sociolinguistic actuality. That is, it is a model, or schema, or mental set, rather than an empirical description of usage. As such, it seems to be a profound, productive, perhaps even self-fulfilling, model. Lawrence seems to me to subscribe to the model (half a century before Bernstein!) and to make his characters conform to it.

families; that is, they are sociological rather than purely linguistic in origin. Once learned, they have different consequences for speakers: the possessor of an elaborated code is allegedly more mobile, less tied to his immediate communicative situation, more able to generalize, to symbolize, more distanced and ironic in the way he relates language to subject-matter, than someone who knows a restricted code only. The restricted code user is limited to the meanings implicit in the immediate situation, and he articulates these allusively, using many pronouns and other pro-forms such as 'thing', 'stuff', 'do', 'get', etc., assuming that his interlocutor will understand what he means. He lacks the coding structures for qualification and exact specification of meanings enjoyed by the elaborated code user. The elaborated code promotes mobility, individuality, authority; the restricted code blocks these kinds of socio-economic advantage. On the cognitive side, the elaborated code is claimed to give access to universalistic or transcendant meanings, whereas the restricted code limits its possessors to particularistic aspects of immediate contexts.

But, in the view of linguists who have criticized Bernstein's theory, these values are double-faced: the advantage is not all on the side of the elaborated code user. If the restricted code limits mobility, making upward departure from a group difficult, it is also an instrument of solidarity within that group, and a medium for intimacy between individuals (remember that it depends on assumptions of shared meanings, therefore closeness of experience); and if the laborated code favours abstract discourse, it can also encourage vacuousness, impersonality and alienation.*

I believe that anyone who is in the least familiar with Lawrence's work will recognize the potential relevance of these ideas to the communicative relationships he builds between his characters. In *Sons and Lovers*, we might regard

* W. Labov, 'The logic of non-standard English', in P. P. Giglioli, ed., *Language and Social Context* (Harmondsworth: Penguin, 1972).

Paul as an elaborated code speaker subject to the strains of a family in which there is a virtually classic conflict between the demands and responsibilities of the two codes. His mother has come down in the world, sacrificing the middle-class values of culture and sensitivity which the elaborated code alone can carry. Her husband Walter may be much more revealingly regarded as a restricted code user than a dialect speaker. Paul's education and his language potential give him the power to free himself from his constricting working class environment, but this same linguistic facility also divides him from his family and friends, whose intimacy, where it exists, is founded on the sharing of a restricted code.

In chapter XI of *Sons and Lovers*, the same one from which I quoted phrases indicating alienated sex, there is a crucial episode in which Paul submits his relationship with Miriam Leivers to a series of severe tests. After many years of sexually distant friendship, Paul, partly against his instincts, sleeps with her; she regards the sexual act as an act of 'sacrifice'; Paul convinces himself that he must give Miriam up; he tells his mother, from whom the affair with Miriam has deeply divided him, that he is going to do this; and announces the rejection to Miriam. The chapter concludes with a precariously affectionate scene reuniting Paul and Mrs Morel.

Now Lawrence's narrator analyses Paul's view of his sexual failure with Miriam in Freudian terms: 'men . . . like himself, bound in by their own virginity . . . so sensitive to their women that they would go without them for ever rather than do them a hurt, an injustice . . . for a woman was like their mother . . .' Perhaps. Another way of looking at Paul and Miriam's estrangement would be to refer it to an incompatability of mind-style, expressed in a conflict of codes. Let us look at the language of their speech and thoughts. After they have first made love, it begins to rain:

'The rain!' he said.

'Yes – is it coming on you?'

She put her hands over him, on his hair, on his shoulders, to feel if the raindrops fell on him. She loved him dearly. He, as he lay with his face on the dead pine-leaves, felt extraordinarily quiet. He did not mind if the raindrops came on him; he would have lain and got wet through: he felt as if nothing mattered, as if his living were smeared away into the beyond, near and quite lovable. This strange, gentle reaching-out to death was new to him.

'We must go,' said Miriam.

'Yes,' he answered, but did not move.

To him now, life seemed a shadow, day a white shadow; night, and death, and stillness, and inaction, this seemed like *being*. To be alive, to be urgent and insistent – that was *not-to-be*. The highest of all was to melt out into the darkness and sway there, identified with the great Being.

'The rain is coming in on us,' said Miriam.

He rose, and assisted her.

'It is a pity,' he said.

'What?'

'To have to go. I feel so still.'

'Still!' she repeated.

'Stiller than I have ever been in my life.'

He was walking with his hand in hers. She pressed his fingers, feeling a slight fear. Now he seemed beyond her; she had a fear lest she should lose him.

'The fir-trees are like presences on the darkness: each one only a presence.'

She was afraid, and said nothing.

'A sort of hush: the whole night wondering and asleep: I suppose that's what we do in death – sleep in wonder.'

She had been afraid before of the brute in him: now of the mystic.

Note that Miriam says very little. What she does say, is either strongly under the control of Paul's language (she responds to what he says, repeating bits of his utterances), or is a direct, pragmatic reaction to the rain; her syntax is entirely uncomplicated, and her vocabulary neutral. In her language, she is related simply to the immediate context. Only one short paragraph ('He was walking . . .') and the beginning of another ('She put her hands . . .') are located within Miriam's consciousness, and those are simple reports of her immediate feelings about Paul.

Paul, on the other hand, expresses himself in speech and thought which both go beyond the situation and are syntactically elaborated. He is detached, strongly conscious of his individual self, using language to project himself out of the situation by symbolism: 'life seemed a shadow, day a white shadow', 'The fir-trees are like presences on the darkness'. Bernstein suggests that 'elaborated codes orient their users towards universalistic meanings, whereas restricted codes orient, sensitize, their users to particularistic meanings', a distinction which seems relevant to the function of discourse in this scene. Particularly in the paragraph beginning 'To him now . . .', Paul's language is analytic and generalizing, transforming his immediate experience into philosophical gestures; the syntactic strategy is to nominalize categories of his experience – 'inaction', 'to be alive' – and equate them with grander generalizations – 'being', 'not-to-be', 'the great Being'. Paul establishes himself through language as a 'mystic'; perhaps Miriam doesn't have this facility for universalization, but at any rate the mystical side of Paul frightens her.

For Paul, the use of an elaborated code is liberating, though it is destructive of their relationship. Later, it frees him completely from his affair with Miriam. The decision to give up Miriam is confirmed in an epiphanic moment of intense symbolism. On the surface, Paul is experiencing the scent of lilies and irises; but the elaborated code user does not respond to the surface of the situation. Here, the brutal eroticism of the metaphors makes it clear that Paul is interpreting the flowers as symbols of his own sexual predicament – his simultaneous desire and revulsion, the strength and cruelty of his desire, and the violence of his revulsion against the grasping but undesiring female:

> He went across the bed of pinks, whose keen perfume came sharply across the rocking, heavy scent of the lilies, and stood alongside the white barrier of flowers. They flagged all loose, as if they were panting. The scent made him drunk. He went down to the field to watch the moon sink under.
>
> A corncrake in the hay-close called insistently. The moon slid quite quickly downwards, growing more flushed. Behind him the great flowers leaned as if they were calling. And then, like a shock, he caught another perfume, something raw and coarse. Hunting round, he found the purple iris, touched their fleshy throats and their dark, grasping hands. At any rate, he had found something. They stood stiff in the darkness. Their scent was brutal. The moon was melting down upon the crest of the hill. It was gone; all was dark. The corncrake called still.
>
> Breaking off a pink, he suddenly went indoors.
>
> 'Come, my boy,' said his mother. 'I'm sure it's time you went to bed.'
>
> He stood with the pink against his lips.
>
> 'I shall break off with Miriam, mother,' he answered calmly.

The elaborated code-user's ability to symbolize, appropriating features of an immediate situation to stand for his feelings about himself and other people, allows him to objectify his problems, to realize what they are and treat them with relative detachment.

Meanwhile, Paul and his mother are divided from one

another by his attachment to Miriam. They hardly speak. 'There was a coldness between him and her'; 'There was between him and his mother a peculiar condition of people frankly finding fault with each other.' These descriptions of their alienation are in elaborated syntax reminiscent of the alienated mind-style of Lambert Strether. 'Coldness' impersonalizes the relationship between them: it is an adjective nominalized, and the effect is to refrain from specifying who was cold – contrast the greater immediacy and evaluative directness of 'Paul was cold' or even 'Paul and his mother were cold towards each other'. 'A peculiar condition' even further neutralizes the relationship; and the syntax, heavily transformed away from direct statement, externalizes the relationship between mother and son, presenting it in terms of '(other) people'. The sentence-structure, typically elaborated, shifts the personal feelings it alludes to away from the participants. Here we have elaborated code as evasion and distance. It is necessary to restore the restricted code as an instrument of intimacy. Since the restricted code relies heavily on implicit meanings, it can only be employed when speakers enjoy shared assumptions and values concerning the topics of discourse. Between Paul and Mrs Morel, this solidarity is re-attained only when Paul has definitively given up Miriam, at the end of the chapter. He returns home, and speaks to his mother:

'I told her,' he said.

'I'm glad,' replied the mother, with great relief.

He hung up his cap wearily.

'I said we'd have done altogether,' he said.

'That's right, my son,' said the mother. 'It's hard for her now, but best in the long run. I know. You weren't suited for her.'

He laughed shakily as he sat down.

'I've had such a lark with some girls in a pub,' he said.

His mother looked at him. He had forgotten Miriam

now. He told her about the girls in the Willow Tree. Mrs Morel looked at him. It seemed unreal, his gaiety. At the back of it was too much horror and misery.

'Now have some supper,' she said very gently.

Afterwards he said wistfully:

'She never thought she'd have me, mother, not from the first, and so she's not disappointed.'

'I'm afraid,' said his mother, 'she doesn't give up hopes of you yet.'

'No,' he said, 'perhaps not.'

'You'll find it's better to have done,' she said.

'*I* don't know,' he said desperately.

'Well, leave her alone,' replied his mother.

The sentences are obviously simple in structure, refraining from elaboration or qualification. Emotions can be hinted at, do not have to be spelled out. The reliance of mother and son on the assumption of shared referents can be observed in the usage of pronouns and of transformational deletions. Paul's first utterance, 'I told her', trusts his mother to supply the identity of 'her' and to recover the deleted complement of 'told' – 'that I was breaking off with her'. The mother continues in the same mode; in her response, she doesn't need to specify what makes her 'glad'; nor, when she says 'It's hard for her now', does she have to indicate what the 'It' abbreviates. The two speakers continue to communicate elliptically, in close sympathy, despite Mrs Morel's recognition of 'horror and misery' behind Paul's good humour. The whole transaction might be taken to demonstrate that the 'restricted code', despite its name, has positive uses as a sign of and promoter of intimacy.

5 THE NOVELIST, THE READER AND THE COMMUNITY

IN this book I have required my readers to adopt what might be called a 'structural' attitude in their thinking about the novel. I began by assuming that a prose fiction text is a certain kind of (abstract) object whose nature can be specified in terms of its elements and their interrelationships. I did not attempt to propose a set of elements which might define the novel as a genre – novels are too diverse for that enterprise, and they draw extensively upon the resources of other kinds of discourse – but rather, I started with components that might be expected to characterize most kinds of text. A two-fold appeal was made to the notion of *sentence* as defined in linguistics. First, I suggested that the elements of novels are structurally analogous to the components of sentences. I have tried to illustrate a modest version of this thesis, namely that concepts such as 'point of view' which critics use in talking about novels can be interpreted in terms of this analogy by referring to correspondent elements in the structure of the sentence. Second, what is surely uncontroversial, the compositional structure of a novel is realized in, and can be studied in, the actual sentences of its linguistic surface. Most of the book has consisted of analyses seeking to demonstrate connections between major compositional elements and details of textual surface structure.

Structural analysis – my approach or anyone else's – focuses on the text as an *object*. That is its purpose: to offer a theory of the object under analysis. I think my theory does this, but also goes further, suggesting ways in which the individual novel or story can be related to the wider contexts of writing and reading and social structure. I want to conclude with some notes on the broader implications of the present theory of textual structure.

My general point is that structures 'in the text' imply patterns of relationships, and systems of knowledge, in the community which has produced the text and its readers. Also, patterns of *activity* are implied: the writer's speech acts, the reader's 'decoding' process. As an illustration, let us return to the notion of 'intertextuality' mentioned in chapter 3 (p. 69). This is the idea that a work is made up from scraps of earlier writings, metaphorically like a palimpsest, a re-used parchment with the half-erased traces of the previous text showing through the lines of new writing. In Brooke-Rose's novel *Thru*, intertextuality takes the form of a fragmentary kind of allusiveness: the book constantly quotes bits of pre-existing language, imitates established styles of writing. It is a patchwork of references and jokes. Consider this fact from the point of view, not of textual structure, but of the implied discourse relationship with the reader. The author makes it very obvious what she is doing, so this is a very active relationship. The reader rapidly learns to be on the alert, watchful lest any references escape his attention. He will not catch every allusion, and some he will only partly understand, or fail to identify precisely. No two individuals have had an identical range of experiences, no two people have exactly the same interests, so this incomplete matching of deep structures is an understandable and typical feature of communication.

However, the novel in question is not a random list of

arbitrary references: it alludes constantly to linguistics, semiology, structuralism, the *nouveau roman*, and to the styles and situations of a modern academic community preoccupied with such topics. For a reader within such a situation, and interested in such subjects (as I am), catching the allusions is not a hit-or-miss affair. He shares with the author a specialized system of information and interest; they belong to the same community. At least (since everyone fulfils many roles, belongs to many groups), their communitymemberships overlap in an appropriate way. Writing and reading, for such individuals, construct a bond in which both parties draw on the shared conventions of the relevant culture.

It is of course the system of conventions which makes possible the work and the arrangements of words within the work. The systematic organization of society (including 'rules' for writing) transcends and controls the individual, determining the verbal patterns s/he can deploy or respond to. *This control applies to the novelist as well as the reader.* S/he can write meaningfully only within the possibilities provided by the systems of conventions which define the culture.

I realize that the prominence I have given to 'convention' produces immediate difficulties for its honoured antithesis, 'creativity'. This seems to me an entirely acceptable outcome: there is no good reason for taking value-terms like 'creativity' on trust, every reason for testing them, for requiring a case to be made out – as I shall attempt to do shortly.

In every communication, whether it is a novel or a casual conversation, a great many diverse systems of knowledge are brought into play. This is another way of saying that texts are exceedingly complex. Writers and speakers have to know the principles upon which sentences are constructed: this is the system of 'linguistic competence' as Chomsky has named it – and he has shown that this is a very substantial and intricate knowledge. Ability to construct and to decode

sentences is not, however, sufficient to explain all the com-
plexities of whole texts. A writer constructs a sequence of
sentences so that they are textually cohesive (see chapter 3)
and also appropriate to the many contexts to which his work
of communication relates. He chooses patterns of language
which encode in conventional ways his community's organization and valuation of their experiences. These choices
are expressed by linguistic patterns which, in any one novel,
signal a diversity of conventions: which obey the novel's
rules for rendering dialogue or dialect, which set a particular
level of formality in the author's voice, which link the text
to earlier works in the same tradition (cf. Storey's *Radcliffe
and the Gothic*), which imitate discourse outside fiction
(cf. *Thru*, *Ulysses*), which suggest a particular occupational
or social group, etc., etc. The novel, like all other texts but
perhaps to a greater degree than many, is 'polysystemic',
drawing its structure from a variety of systems of codes which
also enter the generation of other texts. Intertextuality is not
a kind of quilting process whereby one work is composed of
fragments of other texts (though literal quotation *may* be involved) but a dependence on multiple codes and thus an
indirect link with other texts that draw on these same
codes.

Interestingly, the same linguistic pattern may relate to
more than one code, either alternatively or simultaneously,
depending on context. An excellent example of simultaneous
coding is provided by the illustrations of 'elaborated code'
quoted from *Sons and Lovers*. The elaborated code which Paul
speaks and thinks is also a literary code originating in the highly
symbolic and emotionally expressive language of literary
Romanticism. His language therefore signifies a compound
of two sets of values at once. One set of values (associated
with the language of high Romanticism) exists largely
within the institution of literature; the other (elaborated
code) is broadly pervasive within English-speaking society
at large. Elaborated vs. restricted is a distinction which is

relevant to speech and writing in a vast range of communicative contexts, most of them non-literary (e.g. the conflict between teachers' and pupils' models of language in schools, between those of managers and of labour-force in industry). So we have also illustrated a further observation, namely that some codes which are responsible for important structural features of novels are basically *non-literary* codes with established social values outside the institution of prose fiction. Two further examples from the literature we have examined already. In connection with semic analysis, I mentioned above (p. 35) that the semes relevant to novels 'tend to reflect the clichés and stereotypes in terms of which the society which supports the literature sees itself'. The semantic features proposed for *The Great Gatsby* surely come into this category: they would be needed to account for the semantic structure of journalistic writings, contemporaneous and modern, about the social and material life of American high society in the twenties. Similarly, the aphoristic generic sentences which I noticed in George Eliot imply a system of sentimental philosophizing that underlies other Victorian writings of a moralizing and inspiring nature. Direct testimony for this observation comes from the work of the Rev. Alexander Main, who extracted a collection of 'Wise, Witty and Tender Sayings' from George Eliot's novels which ran to several hundred pages and several editions during the novelist's lifetime. So the contemporary reader would probably have approached the novels with an already developed receptiveness to this kind of philosophizing voice. It is probably fair to say that the moralizing code, which we first observed as a structural feature of the novels, in fact formed part of the complex of communicative conventions which defined the culture of the reading middle classes in the mid- to later-nineteenth century. Whether this was the case, is a question for sociolinguistic investigation – as is elaborated code, or the semantics of the Jazz Age, or the in-jokes of the structuralist academic community. In all cases,* we can reasonably postulate that structures in the text correlate with systems of experience and values transcending the individual work, and vital to the community against which the work is generated. Structural analysis and contextual analysis can be integrated; and I would like us to think of structural analysis as *essentially* a point of entry into the interpretative activity of setting a work within the community's framework of values.

The mode of structural analysis I have proposed invites and demands close description of linguistic structure. The connection I have made with the language of cultural values directs our attention to specific aspects of linguistic structure: my category *discourse* is the central notion here. The sociolinguistics of discourse is a rich area for development in linguistics, and I hope I have suggested that it can make an original contribution to studies in the sociology of the novel.

Let us move, finally, from social dimensions of text structure to those which concern the individual. In actual fact, I have already hinted at some relevant features of the individual. Just as fictional 'characters' are clusters of semes drawn from various codes, so a real person can be seen, as the social psychologist sees him, as a construction of roles acquired, through the process of socialization, from the vast and systematic repertoire of roles which reside in the culture as a whole. The individual's presentation of himself is coded, and he also has a stock of knowledge which allows him to read the codes in the behaviour of others and in the texts of the various media of his society. The reader's encounter with the text consists basically of the release of knowledge through response to the patterns which the author has

---

* I should add that this definitely includes those codes which are *essentially* literary (Romantic metaphors, structures of sonnets, etc.) : these are sociolinguistic facts just as much as are those codes whose origin seems to be non-literary (restricted code, dialect, occupational register, etc.).

deployed in encoding the deep structure of the work. It is an act of discovery of that which he is already equipped, by his place in the community of readers, to discover. The novel he reads is part of the self-same system of signs to which he personally belongs.

Or, the same in many respects. As we have seen, there is no complete matching of experiences, no absolute identity of role-repertoires. If we all possessed exactly the same knowledge, there would be no point in communicating. Society is vaster than the individual, and so is history. Novelists, like other people, need to pass on what is special in their own particular knowledge. This communication may be possible within the possibilities afforded by existing formal conventions, and in such a case we may speak of a limited kind of creativity. The analogy of transformational-generative grammar may again be helpful. Chomsky has argued that language allows its users to produce and comprehend an infinite number of different sentences, on the basis of a finite resource of linguistic knowledge. Since we are finite organisms, we can naturally possess only a limited amount of knowledge. Yet it seems that we constantly produce and understand *new* sentences. (Demonstrations of how this is achieved will be found in Chomsky's writings.) Working in sentences, the novelist of course has access to this facility.

Now the principle of 'infinite use of finite means' almost certainly extends also to other systems of formal knowledge than the competence to produce new sentences. For instance, it seems likely that the stylistic codes, i.e. significant concentrations of specific kinds of structure such as characterize elaborated code, or Gothic, or the symbolic codes of Romanticism, possess the potential for infinite extension. So the novelist can (while he remains content with the linguistic systems at his disposal) say new things, in sentences that his reader will not have encountered before, and within existing stylistic conventions.

Innovation on the basis of existing resources is possible at the level of *content* too. Propp's analysis of the syntax of plot structure may be regarded as a generative system. A large number of combinations of his 'functions of the dramatis personae' may be formed, and there is no predictable limit on the characters that may be invented to fill the roles (cf. pp. 29, 33 above). Thus, the story-teller may construct a very large number of tales (to put it modestly) out of the possibilities provided by a very simple system of available plot-structures. A similar generative facility may exist at the level of thematic organization. Literary historians have noticed variants of the same themes cropping up time and time again in different works over the centuries: the mutability of life, the threat of the unknown, comfort of the home, spring reawakening, wisdom of age and so on. Obviously there are innumerable narratives and situations which can express these themes (or 'topoi' as they are called), and countless surface structure phrasings to articulate detailed statements and symbolizations of them.

I suggest that processes such as the above – working in a much more highly elaborated way than I have been able to evoke – constitute the basis of 'creativity' in fictional writing. The novelist needs to draw simultaneously on a vast battery of codes as s/he constructs the sentences which give shape to his or her ideas. These codes are founded in systems which are 'productive': an unlimited number of rearrangements of a stock of elements is possible. In the finished work, the complex intersection of realizations from a very large number of underlying systems disguises the essentially rule-governed nature of the generation of fictional texts. The reader comes to the published novel equipped with more or less expertise in the underlying systems, gained and consolidated through encounters with other realizations of them. The novel is new to him, but he already enjoys competence in the systems out of which it has been derived. The main work of the novelist is extending the range of creations formed from the existing systems; the chief gain of the reader, the delight of extending his experience of the potentialities of these systems.

Finally, there are more radical kinds of 'creativity', which entail changes in the stock of formal possibilities available to novelists, rather than rearrangements within existing forms. Language itself develops, of course. As a result of cumulative small and gradual changes – probably unnoticed minute differences in the form in which infants learn their mother tongue – the language is progressively reshaped, so that our linguistic competence is now very different from Shakespeare's, even more so from Chaucer's, and almost unrecognizably different from Anglo-Saxon. The same fluidity is found in the second-order semiological systems which are encoded in language (those at least which display historical continuity, as the novel does). Very small linguistic transformations of elements of the system may be introduced quietly, perhaps fortuitously, and may then develop into important new channels of expression and even pave the way for more profound innovations. A case in point might be 'free indirect style' (see p. 102 above). There is usually no explicit sentence-structure sign that free indirect style, rather than narrative report, is being used. If the text says 'She was tired' ('Eveline', from Joyce's *Dubliners*, 1914), we can't be immediately sure whether this is the narrator describing Eveline's state, or Eveline thinking 'I am tired.' Subsequent sentences continue this surface-structure ambivalence, but the context resolves them as free indirect thought. The point is that this innovation in discourse (whenever it occurred) took place without any major change in the structure of the language; but once accepted, it constituted a fundamental development in the rendering of speech and consciousness. Special (optional) structures, such as the already mentioned combination of present and past, were developed: '*Now* she *was* going to go away like the others, to leave her home' a few sentences later in 'Eveline'.

And the development of indirect free thought in nineteenth-century fiction surely prepared the way for the more revolutionary changes in modes of representing consciousness early in the twentieth century.

'Revolutionary' creativity is a more visible phenomenon (though not *necessarily* more important) in the history of the novel. This may take the form of importing new conventions, new systems, into the novel, for example the creation of the Gothic genre by incorporating a new set of clichés of behaviour and atmosphere, or the controversial (at the time) Naturalist movement making explicit reference to 'sordid' topics which had not previously figured so openly in fiction; or the psychological innovations of Joyce, Woolf, etc., attended by their specialized syntactic conventions for the representation of thought; or the more disturbing formal experiments of Neo-Modernism making a direct assault on the way in which the conventional nineteenth century novel was put together (Beckett, the *nouveau roman*, loose-leaf novels in boxes, etc.). Because I am not writing a history of the European novel, I cannot go into detail on these formal changes. But I hope it will be seen that we are dealing with a type of creative innovation which works essentially *in relation to* the principles of structural organization which exist in the writer, the reader and the community before the change is initiated: a gap exists to be filled by a new system, or a system exists to be upturned, radically transformed, by a writer who feels that the change can make new meanings available to his community. A parallel kind of radical transformation is illustrated by poets such as Dylan Thomas and e. e. cummings, who write against the established regularities of the grammar, creating an anti-grammar of their own. In the grammar of fiction, as well as the grammar of poetry, the impact of new principles of formal organization is felt, in the reader's experience, as a shock against the existing formal systems of which she possesses knowledge. The new systems may then be absorbed as the norm. The process of formal change may be described in structural terms, and as we have seen, the structural description is an exposition of factors intimately and vitally relevant to the individual (writer and reader) and his community.

FURTHER READING

I HAVE aimed to outline a new approach, drawing on a variety of sources in linguistics and criticism. The eclecticism and the newness of this approach mean that the reader will not find other works which consistently employ exactly the same terms and methods; the following recommendations for further reading represent the range of sources from which I have drawn my ideas.

Linguistics

A comprehensive general introduction to linguistic theory covering most basic notions in the discipline and neutral in its own orientation is J. Lyons, *Introduction to Theoretical Linguistics* (London: Cambridge University Press, 1968). Lyons, ed., *New Horizons in Linguistics* (Harmondsworth: Penguin, 1970) is an informative collection of original essays on most aspects of linguistics; theory and application. Other introductions include V. Fromkin and R. Rodman, *An Introduction to Language* (New York: Holt, Reinhart & Winston, 2nd edn, 1978); R. Fowler, *Understanding Language* (London: Routledge & Kegan Paul, 1974). A more recent introduction with a similar range is J. Lyons, *Language and Linguistics* (Cambridge: Cambridge University Press, 1981).

Some of the best introductory books are based on the transformational-generative model of grammar. An enthusiastic work which introduces generative linguistics in the context of the psychology of language is J. Aitchison, *The Articulate Mammal* (London: Hutchinson, 1976). N. Smith and D. Wilson, *Modern Linguistics: The Results of Chomsky's Revolution* (Harmondsworth: Penguin, 1979) is particularly recommended as an introduction to the thinking behind, and the implications of, TG. Of several textbooks on the transformational analysis of syntax, the best is A. Akmajian and F. Heny, *An Introduction to the Principles of Transformational Syntax* (Cambridge, Mass.: MIT Press, 1975). More recent versions of TG are the subject of A. Radford, *Transformational Syntax* (Cambridge: Cambridge University Press, 1981). For an eclectic reference grammar to the transformational syntax of English, consult R. P. Stockwell, P. Schachter and B. H. Partee, *The Major Syntactic Structure of English* (New York: Holt, Rinehart & Winston, 1973). A modern non-transformational grammar widely referred to by linguistic stylisticians is R. Quirk, S. Greenbaum, G. Leech and J. Svartvik, *A Grammar of Contemporary English* (London: Longman, 1972).

Chomsky's own work, which is often technical and difficult, is best sampled in relation to the textbooks cited above. His important early books are *Syntactic Structures* (The Hague: Mouton, 1957) and *Aspects of the Theory of Syntax* (Cambridge, Mass.: MIT Press, 1965). More recent books include *Reflections on Language* (London: Temple Smith, 1976); *Rules and Representations* (New York: Columbia University Press, 1979 and Oxford: Blackwell, 1980). The importance of Chomsky's ideas is colossal: not only the specific tools of syntactic analysis which he offers, but also his general philosophy of language and thought, has had a great influence on stylistic and structuralist research into literature.

The other individual linguist whose relevance to linguistic

criticism must be acknowledged is M. A. K. Halliday. Halliday's 'functional' model is particularly valuable because it proposes that choices of linguistic structure are motivated, can be explained with reference to social and interpersonal functions. Halliday's own *Introduction to Functional Linguistics* is forthcoming (1983). Useful collections of his papers are published as *Explorations in the Functions of Language* (London: Edward Arnold, 1973); *Halliday: System and Function in Language* (London: Oxford University Press, 1976), ed. G. R. Kress with a useful introduction; *Language as Social Semiotic* (London: Edward Arnold, 1978). The standard work on the 'textual' function is M. A. K. Halliday and R. Hasan, *Cohesion in English* (London: Longman, 1976).

Sociolinguistics – as a distinct part of linguistics – is the subject of several helpful introductory textbooks, for instance P. Trudgill, *Sociolinguistics* (Harmondsworth: Penguin, 1974); R. A. Hudson, *Sociolinguistics* (Cambridge: Cambridge University Press, 1980). The most relevant collection of papers on sociolinguistics, from various perspectives, is P. P. Giglioli, ed., *Language and Social Context* (Harmondsworth: Penguin, 1972) – see especially the contributions by Searle on speech acts, Bernstein on class and codes, and Labov who presents a critique of Bernstein. Bernstein's earlier and more provocative papers on 're-stricted and elaborated codes' are collected in *Class, Codes and Control* Vol. I (London: Routledge & Kegan Paul, 1971), while Labov's main researches on the correlation of language variety and social stratification can be found in *Sociolinguistic Patterns* ((Philadelphia: University of Pennsylvania Press, 1972).

The main linguistic features relevant to face-to-face inter-action (as distinct from broader sociolinguistic patterns) are surveyed in M. Coulthard, *Introduction to Discourse Analysis* (London: Longman, 1977).

Linguistic stylistics or linguistic criticism

General introductions from various points of view include A. Cluysenaar, *Introduction to Literary Stylistics* (London: Batsford, 1976) (mostly on language and the perception of literary form in poetry: contains some excellent practical criticism); R. Chapman, *Linguistic and Literature* (London: Edward Arnold, 1973); G. N. Leech, *A Linguistic Guide to English Poetry* (London: Longman, 1969); G. W. Turner, *Stylistics* (Harmondsworth: Penguin, 1973); H. G. Widdowson, *Stylistics and the Teaching of Literature* (London: Longman, 1975).

The best theoretical and practical studies have been published as short papers rather than books, but many of these are very accessible since they have been printed or reprinted in anthologies. Some of the earlier anthologies, which contain seminal papers for theory or methodology, are T. A. Sebeok, ed., *Style in Language* (Cambridge, Mass.: MIT Press, 1960) (NB the paper by Jakobson first published in Sebeok); S. B. Chatman, ed., *Literary Style: A Symposium* (London and New York: Oxford University Press, 1971), containing an important article by Halliday, 'Linguistic Function and Literary Style'; Chatman, ed., *Approaches to Poetics* (New York: Columbia University Press, 1973); Chatman and S. R. Levin, eds, *Essays on the Language of Literature* (Boston: Houghton-Mifflin, 1967); D. C. Freeman, ed., *Linguistics and Literary Style* (New York: Holt, Rinehart & Winston, 1970) – perhaps the most representative collection, containing some of the most frequently referred to and influential papers; B. B. Kachru and F. W. Stahlke, eds, *Current Trends in Stylistics* (Edmonton: Linguistic Research, Inc., 1972); G. A. Love and M. Payne, eds, *Contemporary Essays on Style* (Glenview, Illinois: Scott, Foresman & Co., 1969).

More recently, see M. K. L. Ching, M. C. Haley and R. F. Lunsford, eds, *Linguistic Perspectives on Literature*

(London: Routledge & Kegan Paul, 1980); D. C. Freeman, ed., *Essays in Modern Stylistics* (London and New York: Methuen, 1981), an anthology which concentrates on applications of transformational linguistics to literary problems. Two recent British collections which emphasize 'discourse' and 'functional' approaches and which are particularly attentive to pedagogic aspects of work in stylistics are R. Carter and D. Burton, eds, *Literary Text and Language Study* (London: Edward Arnold, 1982) and R. Carter, ed., *Language and Literature: An Introductory Reader in Stylistics* (London: George Allen & Unwin, 1982).

I have written, or edited and contributed to, several collections of papers in linguistics criticism: Fowler, ed., *Essays on Style and Language* (London: Routledge & Kegan Paul, 1966); *The Languages of Literature* (London: Routledge & Kegan Paul, 1971); *Style and Structure in Literature* (Oxford: Blackwell, 1975); *Literature as Social Discourse* (London: Batsford, 1981). Readers interested in the development of the subject will detect quite significant changes of orientation and method over those fifteen years.

Although there has been a great deal of linguistic study of poetry, and some of drama (e.g. D. Burton, *Dialogue and Discourse* (London: Routledge & Kegan Paul, 1980)), linguistic critics have only recently begun to turn their attention to the novel. For a more traditional stylistic approach to the novel, see S. Ullmann, *Style in the French Novel* (Oxford: Blackwell, 2nd edn, 1964). The greater power and technicality of modern linguistics is reflected in W. J. M. Bronzwaer, *Tense in the Novel* (Groningen: Wolters-Noordhoff, 1970), which contains a useful discussion of free indirect style – on which subject see also Brian McHale, 'Free Indirect Discourse: A Survey of Recent Accounts,' *PTL*, 3 (1978), 249–87. A more conservative linguistic study, but useful, is N. Page, *Speech in the English Novel* (London: Longman, 1973). Seymour Chatman has contributed notably to the linguistic study of prose fiction: see his *The Later Style of Henry James* (Oxford: Blackwell, 1972) (mainly a transformational approach to the syntax); 'The Structure of Narrative Transmission' in Fowler, ed., *Style and Structure in Literature; Story and Discourse: Narrative Structure in Fiction and Film* (Ithaca and London: Cornell University Press, 1978). G. N. Leech and M. H. Short, *Style in Fiction* (London: Longman, 1981) is a comprehensive work which complements the present book.

Some impressive Russian work on the language of fiction has appeared in English translation: M. Bakhtin, *Problems of Dostoevsky's Poetics* (Ann Arbor: Ardis, 1973); B. A. Uspensky, *A Poetics of Composition* (Berkeley and Los Angeles: University of California Press, 1973); V. N. Voloshinov, *Marxism and the Philosophy of Language* (New York: Seminar Press, 1973). The work of Bakhtin and his disciples concentrates on the fascinating idea of 'dialogic' or 'polyphonic' structure in fiction, the notion that the sentences constructed for a novel's implied author encode an interplay of voices, and thus of values, between himself and the consciousness and moral position of his characters. A. K. Zholkovsky and Yu. K. Scheglov, *Generating the Literary Text*, is a study of the possibility of synthesizing texts from thematic materials. For fuller exemplification of work of this kind, see L. M. O'Toole, *Structure, Style and Interpretation in the Russian Short Story* (New Haven and London: Yale University Press, 1982).

'Structuralism' and the structural analysis of narrative

'Structuralism' refers to a broad set of intellectual habits in the human sciences, and more specifically, in this context, to theories of poetic and narrative structure which were current, particularly in France, in the 1960s. The intellectual ancestry of this movement is complex. Main progenitor of structuralist theory was Ferdinand de Saussure: see J. Culler, *Saussure* (London: Fontana, 1976). As far as literary applications of structuralist thought were concerned, the Russian 'Formalists' of the 1920s provided a theoretical foundation. Pioneer Russian formalist writings can be found in L. T. Lemon and M. J. Reis, eds, *Russian Formalist Criticism* (Lincoln, Nebraska: University of Nebraska Press, 1965) and in L. Matejka and K. Pomorska, eds, *Readings in Russian Poetics* (Cambridge, Mass.: MIT Press, 1971). A classic statement of structuralist/formalist theory applied to poetry is Roman Jakobson's paper 'Linguistics and Poetics' in the Sebeok collection referred to in the previous section. T. Bennett, *Formalism and Marxism* (London and New York: Methuen, 1979) gives an illuminating perspective on Russian formalism.

There are a number of helpful introductions to the structuralist movement. D. Robey, ed., *Structuralism: An Introduction* (London: Oxford University Press, 1973) reprints a series of popular lectures on structuralism in various disciplines. For structuralism and literature, see J. Culler, *Structuralist Poetics* (London: Routledge & Kegan Paul, 1975), a suggestive, critical account, with a full discussion of the various uses of linguistic models in literary studies, and an extensive bibliography; T. Hawkes, *Structuralism and Semiotics* (London: Methuen, 1977) is very suitable as a first introduction to the subject; see also R. Scholes, *Structuralism in Literature* (New Haven: Yale University Press, 1974).

The model for structuralist analysis of narrative is Vladimir Propp's proposal of 1927 that plot structures of individual narratives can be analysed as conventional sequences of elements found in other works of the same genre. See his *Morphology of the Folktale* (Austin, Texas: University of Texas Press, 1968). The model was fruitful in the structural analysis of myth: see P. Maranda, ed., *Mytholgy* (Harmondsworth: Penguin, 1972). In narratology, such influential literary scholars and linguistics as Barthes, Todorov and Greimas adapted it to apply it to a variety of narrative forms from short fiction to epistolary novels. Readers of French should consult a special issue of the journal *Communications*, 8 (1966) in which two crucial, programmatic essays by Barthes and by Todorov appeared. Barthes' essay is translated as 'Introduction to the structural analysis of narratives' in R. Barthes, *Image-Music-Text: Essays Selected and Translated by Stephen Heath* (London: Fontana, 1977). Chatman applies Barthes' technique to Joyce's story 'Eveline' in 'New ways of analyzing narrative structure', *Language and Style*, 2 (1969). Other relevant works by Barthes include *Elements of Semiology* (London: Cape, 1967) for his version of Saussurean semiological theory; *Mythologies* (London: Cape, 1972), a highly readable and entertaining set of essays on the semiology of modern popular culture and the media; and *S/Z* (Paris: Seuil, 1970) – fascinating analysis of a story by Balzac, which is best read in French, but is available also in an English translation by R. Miller (London: Cape, 1975). A typical work by Todorov is *Littérature et signification* (Paris: Larousse, 1967). Two of Todorov's other books have been translated by Richard Howard: *The Fantastic* (Ithaca: Cornell University Press, 1975) and *The Poetics of Prose* (Ithaca: Cornell University Press, 1977).

Criticism and theory of fiction

Mark Schorer's essay 'Technique as discovery', referred to in ch. 1, was first published in *The Hudson Review*, 1948, and has been reprinted in several anthologies including D. Lodge, ed., *Twentieth Century Literary Criticism* (London: Longman, 1972).

A selection of important literary-critical works which relate to the present book would include at least the following:

M. Allott, ed., *Novelists on the Novel* (London: Routledge & Kegan Paul, 1959) – novelists' own views on the aims and techniques of fiction; E. Auerbach, *Mimesis* (Princeton: Princeton University Press, 1953) – a classic presentation of the relation between language and world-view; M. Bloomfield, ed., *The Interpretation of Narrative* (Cambridge, Mass.: Harvard University Press, 1970); W. C. Booth, *The Rhetoric of Fiction* (Chicago: University of Chicago Press, 1961) which is responsible for a number of important critical terms such as 'implied author' and 'unreliable narrator'; J. Halperin, ed., *The Theory of the Novel: New Essays* (London and New York: Oxford University Press, 1974); B. Hardy, *The Appropriate Form* (London: Athlone Press, 1964); W. Iser, *The Implied Reader* (Baltimore: Johns Hopkins University Press, 1974) an original account of the way fiction is designed to be filled out by an involved reader; D. Lodge, *Language of Fiction* (London: Routledge & Kegan Paul, 1966), a critic's rather than a linguist's view of language, but a book which paved the way for more technical linguistic studies of fiction; R. Scholes and R. Kellogg, *The Nature of Narrative* (London and New York: Oxford University Press, 1966) for fictional structures in the light of the earlier history of narrative; F. Stanzel, *Narrative Situations in the Novel* (Bloomington: Indiana University Press, 1969); P. Stevick, ed., *Theory of the Novel* (New York: Free Press, 1967) containing many valuable and influential twentieth-century pioneer articles working towards theories of fiction.

Theory of fiction has much advanced since the first edition of the present book, in 1977, stimulated largely by intellectual developments in structuralism, semiotics, linguistics and other progressive disciplines. The following is a selection of titles from recent years:

D. Cohn, *Transparent Minds: Narrative Modes for Presenting Consciousness in Fiction* (Princeton: Princeton University Press, 1978); W. Iser, *The Act of Reading: A Theory of Aesthetic Response* (London: Routledge & Kegan Paul, 1978); U. Eco, *The Role of the Reader: Explorations in the Semiotics of Texts* (Bloomington and London: Indiana University Press, 1979); G. Genette, *Narrative Discourse* (Oxford: Blackwell, 1980); F. Jameson, *The Political Unconscious: Narrative as a Socially Symbolic Act* (London: Methuen, 1981); S. S. Lanser, *The Narrative Act: Point of View in Prose Fiction* (Princeton: Princeton University Press, 1981); H. Ruthrof, *The Reader's Construction of Narrative* (London: Routledge & Kegan Paul, 1981); H. Bonheim, *The Narrative Modes: Techniques of the Short Story* (Cambridge: Brewer, 1982); G. Prince, *Narratology: The Form and Functioning of Narrative* (The Hague: Mouton, 1982).

Journals in linguistic criticism and in literary theory

Critical Inquiry, Criticism, Diacritics, Essays in Poetics, Journal of Literary Semantics, Language and Style, New Literary History, Poetics, Poetics Today (formerly *Poetics and the Theory of Literature, 'PTL'*), *Style, Text*.

INDEX